AFTER THE WALLS CAME DOWN

after the WALLS came DOWN

Discovering Contemporary Relevance
in the Visions of Zechariah 1-6

MARC PALADINO

MASTER PRESS

Published by Master Press

AFTER THE WALLS CAME DOWN

Discovering Contemporary Relevance in the Visions of Zechariah 1-6

published by Master Press

*Unless otherwise specified, the uses of italics or brackets appearing
in all cited works are for this author's emphasis or clarification.*

Printed in the United States

AFTER THE WALLS CAME DOWN

Discovering Contemporary Relevance in the Visions of Zechariah 1-6

ISBN 978-0-9834326-1-6

For information:
MASTER PRESS
3405 ISLAND BAY WAY, KNOXVILLE, TN 37931
Mail to: publishing@ masterpressbooks.com

DEDICATION

To Judy, my precious wife,
sister in the Lord, partner, and friend -
whose editorial gifts helped to turn
my musings into something remotely sensible.
Without God's grace
manifested through her love, patience, and support,
this would not have been possible.

CONTENTS

PUBLISHER'S FOREWORD

It has been a uniquely pleasant experience reading this manuscript for at least two reasons (there are undoubtedly more). The first one is personal; my own deep friendship with the author over many decades has meant that I am personally aware of the richness of his biblical insights. For a long time I have personally looked forward to the day when I might hold in my hand a Marc Paladino title. That that day has come fills me with great delight. Having sat under his teaching ministry over the years, I have been aware that he had far more to give the body of Christ than the spoken word would ever allow. For that reason, I am persuaded that this is only the first of many titles to flow from his pen (keyboard).

The second reason is that Marc has the unique ability to help believers understand the grammatical/historical approach to the study of the Scriptures. Sitting under a Paladino sermon, one realizes that they have gained more than an understanding of a particular biblical topic, but a new perspective on the whole of Scripture! Marc possesses the ability to help people see the interrelatedness of the entire Bible, regardless of which section he is dealing with. Such an approach is vitally needed in an age where people often approach the Bible and "miss the forest for the trees." This is so needed in a day when there is a great dearth of studying the Scripture as a unified whole rather than a compendium of spiritual topics.

The Bible reader will see that perfectly displayed in this work which deals with the early visions of Zechariah. What seemed strange and mysterious at first (one's initial impression of these visions) begins to make perfect sense when placed within its proper historical context. This book is worth it alone for its help in understanding the Exhilic and Post-Exhilic periods of Israel's history. Reading it, I felt myself compelled to study more fully all of the biblical literature dealing with this period.

The real value of this book, though, is in its application of the principles of exile and reorientation to the spiritual journey of the believer today. Reading it, I was able to apply it to my own present circumstances in such a way that I derived immediate encouragement. This is exactly where all study of God's Word should lead us. Too many scholarly works lack this kind of rugged application which biblical study should always yield. I am convinced that the reader of this work will not only learn much about the visions of Zechariah, but also how all God-breathed Scripture is profitable for "teaching, reproof, correction, training in righteousness" (II Timothy 3:17). This work demonstrates that in-depth study of Scripture is far from a mere intellectual exercise but yields rich practical insights for fruitful Christian living.

So it is with great joy that I commend this present work. I am excited to know that Marc's unique insights will now be enjoyed by a wider audience. I am sure that after reading it, you will long to read further works from his pen. May God use this present work to help many to see how God has always used exile and reorientation as his way of building the character of His Son in those he has redeemed.

Neil Silverberg

PREFACE

Walls are not necessarily a bad thing. They provide a defense from the weather and unwanted intruders, as well as some occasionally needed privacy. In the world of the ancient near east, city walls gave definition to places such as Babylon, Jericho, and Jerusalem. One of the last scenes of the *Book of Revelation* describes the beautiful walls of the *New* Jerusalem:

> And he carried me away in the Spirit to a great and high mountain, and showed me the holy city, Jerusalem, coming down out of heaven from God, having the glory of God. Her brilliance was like a very costly stone, as a stone of crystal-clear jasper. It had a *great and high wall*, with twelve gates, and at the gates twelve angels; and names were written on them, which are the names of the twelve tribes of the sons of Israel (Revelation 21:10-12).

Whatever interpretive position one might hold regarding this city, two things are apparent. First, *the city has walls*, which give her distinction so that she stands out in the world. Second, *those walls are transparent*, so that only the beauty that emanates from within is visible. The key to her beauty is her transparency. Transparency allows the glory of God to be visible.

Walls, both visible and invisible, circumscribe our paradigms – those philosophical or theoretical frameworks constructed to provide certitudes which include definitions of the world, our own identity, and that of others. Money, career, culture, nationality, religion, race, and gender are just a few of the building blocks that make up these impenetrable human fortresses. However, once we receive the risen Christ, we soon learn that we have also encountered a new and *alternative* rendering of reality. The things that once defined us are no longer valid. Old familiar passages teach us that all things have become new and we must not remain conformed to the old life patterns and modes of thinking:

> So that if anyone is in Christ, *there is a new creation:* everything old has passed away; see, everything has become new! (2 Corinthians 5:17 NRSV).

> Therefore I urge you, brethren, by the mercies of God, to present your bodies a living and holy sacrifice, acceptable to God, which is your spiritual service of worship. And do not be conformed to this world, but be transformed by the renewing of your mind, so that you may prove what the will of God is, that which is good and acceptable and perfect (Romans 12:1-2).

Paul explained in Second Corinthians that *everything* old has passed away. To many of us, our testimony is one of newness of life in Christ which means we were freed from *socially unacceptable* sins and addictions. However, we have not understood that acquired, culturally conditioned, and deeply entrenched norms must be torn down as well if the kingdom of God is truly going to be established in the hearts, minds, and lives of his people. More than any other means, it is the process of *exile* that God uses to tear down those norms in order to rebuild our lives, or for that matter, whole communities, to reflect an entirely new image – that of Christ. This necessity of exile is illustrated in Jeremiah 48, where Moab is seen as rooted in the typical human characteristics of arrogance and self-sufficiency. God's process to deal with it is as follows:

> "Moab has been at ease since his youth;
> He has also been undisturbed, like wine on its dregs,

And he has not been emptied from vessel to vessel,
Nor has he gone into exile.
Therefore he retains his flavor,
And his aroma has not changed."
"Therefore behold, the days are coming," declares the LORD,
"when I will send to him those who tip vessels, and they will tip
him over, and they will empty his vessels and shatter his jars."
(Jeremiah 48:11-12).

The prophet used the ancient art of wine-making to vividly illustrate God's purging process. As the dregs settled to the bottom of the wineskin, the wine was filtered into new skins, leaving the old sediments behind. This process was repeated until the wine was fit for use. For Moab, their pride and arrogance was the *flavor* to be left behind. The pouring into new skins describes the uncomfortable process of exile. The displacement is experienced in the liminal or transitional state when, for a moment (or season), *there is no wineskin*. The wine is suspended between the two skins while it is being poured. Once the filtered wine has entered the new wineskin there is a *crisis of reorientation* - getting acquainted with a new situation. This crisis of reorientation is at the heart of Zechariah's visions in Chapters 1-6 of his great prophecy, as well as a foundational premise of this book.

MY PERSONAL STORY

The content of this work was born out of my own personal crisis, when everything pertaining to my former life began crumbling to the ground. I first encountered the Lord Jesus in 1971, in an authentic, life-altering salvation experience. About ten years later, as a result of some very poor choices in a time of crisis, *the walls* - the things that surrounded and defined my Christian life and identity - came crashing down like those of the ancient besieged city of Jerusalem. The outcome of that crisis was a departure from the Lord that would last 20 years; my own period of *exile*. Those years in darkness were spent building a career as a quality assurance consultant, and in spite of some very difficult early years, the latter were characterized by a pretty good salary, opportunities to travel the world, and a fairly impressive resumé of accomplishments.

When God had seen enough of my foolishness, his incomparable grace miraculously brought an end to the exile in January of 2002. Strangely, however, a year or so after coming back to the Lord, I lost my career, and everything in my life began to unravel. This included the eventual loss of my home and savings and being forced to work on-and-off for low hourly wages in small, Detroit-area businesses. By the grace of God, a Christian couple made their modest rental home available to me. Although I was extremely appreciative of their generosity, the home was in a lower income and racially mixed neighborhood very near the city of Detroit, which (I embarrassingly admit) heightened my sense of uncertainty and vulnerability. I was a "new" Christian again - alive from the dead to be sure, but very weak in the Lord - and like Lazarus, still shrouded in grave clothes. Needless to say, the time had come to earnestly seek the Lord for understanding about what was happening in my life. The wine was being filtered and poured, but into *what*, I hadn't a clue.

As a Bible teacher, God most often speaks to my heart through new understandings of the Scriptures. I am not one to hear voices, and actually envy people who seem to "hear" God tell them what to do. I pass no judgment on anyone, but personally tend to err on the side of caution in such matters. That being said, very early one morning while sitting on the bedroom floor, waiting quietly on the Lord, I was trying desperately to get a perspective on these recent events. What was most difficult to understand was that I was willing to *voluntarily give it all away* if that was what God wanted of me. Why was it necessary to suffer the indignity of *having it all taken*? I would later learn that the voluntary surrender of our goods can take place with *pride* in our hearts (in a generous, yet condescending manner). Contrarily, to have it all taken away by circumstances out of our control is unmistakably humbling and oppressive. The experience brings to us the capacity for better understanding the humiliation of those who are marginalized and oppressed, if only in a small way. It changes how we relate to others in both life and ministry – a lesson that has proven valuable to me in the church body where I was planted. In our neighborhood at *Lord of the Harvest*, we are confronted with broken and marginalized people on a daily basis – and they can see through our disingenuous condescension like a plate glass window.

That morning, there were no words to utter. Waiting patiently and quietly - an hour or so passed. Then suddenly, two unforgettable words gently pierced my heart and mind. They weren't *audible*, but I felt them resonating deep in my inner man. The words were "identity reconstruction." At that moment the Spirit of God seemed to be saying: "I am remaking you. I am wiping away everything you thought you were as a man, and I am going to create in you a new identity." Needless to say, that encounter had a powerfully transforming impact that relieved much of the anxiety of the circumstances in which I had found myself. However, in spite of that, there remained a deep desire to more fully understand what it all meant. Little did I realize the journey into truth that had just begun.

A CRISIS OF REORIENTATION

Not long after that experience, while reading the *Book of Zechariah*, I was deeply drawn to the strange and enigmatic visions of chapters 1-6. At first glance, they made no sense at all. This prompted an extended season of research in order to better understand them. Unpacking the series of visions, it became evident that the prophet was being taught by God concerning a *redefinition of Israel's identity* two generations after her city and temple walls had been mercilessly torn down, and her inhabitants suffered the indignity of displacement. It seemed to have a strange correspondence to what was happening in my life, my own experience being obviously on a smaller, personal scale. It was a *crisis of reorientation* - a preparation for a new paradigm.

Although the idea of exile may seem far removed from the modern world, it is not actually difficult to grasp. It is not unusual for individuals, families, or communities to experience a crisis that results in the dissolution of something of great value and the accompanying physical or emotional displacement from what has been comfortable and familiar. This is typically attended by the sense of significant humiliation and/or loss. When this occurs, the idea of exile is experienced in some measure. However, the visions of Zechariah are not really about the experience of *exile*. His prophecies are *post*-exilic, that is to say, *after Israel's period of exile in Babylon*. They deal with the rebuilding process that must begin when the crisis of loss is behind and the *crisis of reorientation* is on the horizon. This crisis brings with it new challenges, insecurities, threats, and temptations to be sure; but also *new possibilities*. The most dangerous challenge of all is the temptation to assume that what was lost must be rebuilt. God's desire however, is that the new orientation be embraced, with its new definitions and his invitation to examine new possibilities for our lives or communities. The response to that invitation will have tremendous bearing on future direction, whether to remain locked in a longing for the past or move forward into the future that God has prepared.

This book is a product of many months of intense engagement with these texts and the impact they have had on my own life. The more I studied them, the clearer the central messages became. The images made sense. The literary structure and the flow of this great prophet's revelation have a way of capturing the imagination. God had taken Zechariah on a journey of images that described the redemptive process of a purposeful God; the one who is *always* actively present among his people, moving them forward and fulfilling his purpose in the world.

Marc Paladino
Spring, 2011

INTRODUCTION

After spending several years studying the *Book of Revelation*, there emerged in my heart a passion for prophetic literary style and imagery. To this I owe a debt of gratitude to David Chilton's great commentary on the *Book of Revelation*, called *The Days of Vengeance* (Chilton 1990). One may or may not agree with all of Chilton's conclusions, but his insightful work has the unique capacity to create in the reader a deep appreciation for the fluid symbolism of the sacred texts. The prophetic style of the Bible is entirely foreign to the cold, logical, and systematic mindset of the modern, western world. For example, to follow an argument on *justification by faith* as presented in Romans by the apostle Paul is reasonably achievable, but when it comes to the prophetic and poetic elements of the Bible, the reader often walks away confused and even bewildered. The sun is often darkened, the moon turns to blood, a woman is complimented on her beautiful teeth because they resemble a flock of sheep, and mountains and trees shout and clap their hands. Unfortunately, we often desperately attempt to interpret these things by either literalizing or by imposing modern categories of thought upon them that the writer could never have imagined. Thus we misinterpret their meaning altogether.

Modern readers of these ancient writings are inevitably confronted with the interpretive challenge of *distance*. We are separated from the world of the text by time, culture, geography, and language, which are among the constituent elements of that distance (Klein, Blomberg, and Hubbard, Jr. 2004:13-17). With no direct and obvious line from the texts of the Bible to our modern context, the challenge exists to place ourselves, at least generally, into the world of the text in order to begin the process of interpretation and re-application, or – as we say, *recontextualization* to the world of the reader. Walter Brueggemann has succinctly articulated the challenge as follows:

> There are, of course, no easy or obvious or exact moves from "then" to "now," and the parallels are necessarily imaginative, impressionistic, and inexact (Brueggemann 2010:11).

The passionate and expressive language of the ancient prophets was intended, by the use of signs and symbols, to evoke the imagination, create mental images, and allow the reader to perceive and experience the truth of God, as James Jordan has said, *Through New Eyes* (Jordan 2000). However, it must always be kept in mind that those images are rooted in and drawn from ancient cultures and worldviews, and require faithful analysis with respect to the elements of *those* cultures. This is, of course, especially true of the Israelite law, temple, and culture, which are the primary essentials of the worldview of biblical authors.

Just as God communicated the *Revelation* to John through the use of signs and symbols, he had also done very much the same to Zechariah and others before him. Both John and Zechariah, though centuries apart, were given relevant information intended to bring assurance of God's presence and victory, in spite of the fact that their contemporary obstacles seemed insurmountable. Although many are at least somewhat familiar with the beastly presence of Imperial Rome when John received his series of visions, relatively few understand the setting and importance of those seen by Zechariah. They were revealed to the prophet during the highly significant, early post-exilic years of rebuilding the nation after its return from the Babylonian Captivity. Remarkably, 2500 years after the fact, the strange visions of this ancient Israelite prophet still provide relevant insights to God's use of *crisis* to reshape his people into the image of his son, the Lord Jesus.

REDEFINITION AND ENLARGEMENT

It is against the backdrop of this little-understood era of Israel's history that the prophet Zechariah saw the series of visions recorded in Zechariah 1-6. It is the premise of this book to illuminate how these visions were given to provide understanding and structure to a people struggling to discover identity and meaning in their new context. It is suggested here that the over-arching message of these visions may be summed up in two words: *redefinition* and *enlargement*. These are critically important keys to understanding the visions of Zechariah, whose writings are arguably among the most difficult to interpret in the Bible. Many significant aspects of the earlier, pre-exilic literature and experience of the nation *appear in Zechariah, yet they are different*. The signs, the symbols, the images, Jerusalem, the temple, the teaching of the law and the former prophets, and even Israel herself are all there, yet strangely altered. They remain unquestionably faithful to the Bible's internal symbolic structure, yet they have been modified, redefined, and recontextualized to suit a new reality that God had prepared for the returned remnant of his people. This redefinition was intended to impact Israel's presence, form, identity, and role in God's redemptive plan. Rather than the exile annihilating forever the identity of the nation, God intended only that it crush the arrogance and private exclusivity of the former city, and give birth to a new and inclusive universality that would become a presence throughout the civilized world. What God revealed to Zechariah speaks of a people coming out of the ashes of displacement, redefined and enlarged, who would bring the knowledge of *Yahweh* (YHWH) to the nations, preparing them, yet unbeknown to them, for the coming of Jesus.

This book is not intended to be an exhaustive commentary. It is my hope that it will, as we examine the history and experience of the nation of Israel, illuminate some things about ourselves and our churches, and especially help us to see God more clearly in times of crisis. Prayerfully, I trust that adequate contextual detail and interpretation has been supplied to give the reader a sense for the application intended herein.

When referring to God, I have elected to randomly use the name *YHWH* – referred to as the *tetragrammation* and best pronounced *Yahweh*. This prominent Old Testament name for God describes him as the self-existent, covenant-keeping God of Israel. Its use is merely intended to draw the reader into the world of the ancient text. May God, through the guidance of the Holy Spirit, open our minds to discover relevant meaning - meaning that may be light in those times of darkness and uncertainty we inevitably face during our earthly journey with him.

ACKNOWLEDGMENTS

An endeavor such as this, or *any* work in the Lord, is never a product of one individual's insight or skill. We are all products of a fellowship or clan of one sort or another, out of which springs a unique *community hermeneutic* – that lens through which our *shared* history and learning has also given us a *shared* interpretation or perspective of Jesus, the Bible, and the mission of God. This book is no exception. *Lord of the Harvest Christian Fellowship*, its family, leadership, and vision has had a positive and significant impact on the content of this work, and the particular lens through which my wife Judy and I view the world. For that, along with the opportunities afforded me by our leadership team, my old and dear friend Neil Silverberg, and the Master Builders network, I am eternally grateful. My appreciation also extends to our church office and food pantry staff, with whom I labored daily for four years – through *the good, the bad, and the ugly*.

I can't pass up this opportunity to boast of a dedicated group of *Bible Orientation Class* students who have supported Judy and me with unwavering loyalty for over five years and counting, even car-pooling down to the city of Detroit to share our class time with a small urban church, *Lord of Lords*, who remain among our dearest friends in Christ. These students have been a core of faithful disciples who weathered many of my new ideas and long-winded nights. Special thanks go to my Senior Pastor and long time friend, Mike "Pastor Oz" Osminski, along with Cindy Vandermarliere and Matt Essian, for the time they invested in reviewing the manuscript. Their constructive comments provided timely encouragement and motivation.

There is yet one more community I wish to acknowledge. It is the fellowship of precious saints in Christ who make up my own family. There are no words to describe the gratitude in my heart for your loving patience and support, especially during those dark years away from the Lord after my own walls came down. With steadfast love you never stopped believing in me, *especially* David and Leah, even though I had given up on myself. You all were, and remain, God's constant reminder to me of his great faithfulness. Now, being gratefully allowed to finish my course, each of you has a share in this small accomplishment. Thank you all:

Judy, Dave, Jen, Leah, Emily, Mom,
Dad (in memoriam), Nancy, Tony, Louise, & Joe

Chapter 1

BACKGROUND
& LITERARY STRUCTURE

The *Preface* proposed that Zechariah 1-6 is about *redefinition and enlargement*. Obviously, in order for something to be *re*defined and enlarged, it must have had an original definition and scope. With that in mind, it is helpful to understand a little of the origin and development of the nation of Israel, and how the state of affairs in Zechariah's time came to be. In fact, in his *Prologue* (Zechariah 1:1-6), the word of the Lord through the mouth of the prophet is inviting us to do precisely that.

ZECHARIAH'S PROLOGUE

In the eighth month of the second year of Darius, the word of the LORD came to Zechariah the prophet, the son of Berechiah, the son of Iddo saying, "The LORD was very angry with your fathers. "Therefore, say to them, 'Thus says the LORD of hosts, "Return to Me," declares the LORD of hosts, "that I may return to you," says the LORD of hosts. "Do not be like your fathers, to whom the former prophets proclaimed, saying, 'Thus says the LORD of hosts, "Return now from your evil ways and from your evil deeds."' But they did not listen or give heed to Me," declares the LORD. "Your fathers, where are they? And the prophets, do they live forever? "But did not My words and My statutes, which I commanded My servants the prophets, overtake your fathers? Then they repented and said, 'As the LORD of hosts purposed to do to us in accordance with our ways and our deeds, so He has dealt with us'" (Zechariah 1:1-6).

A PRIESTLY KINGDOM

Israel was "born" 1500 years before the time of Zechariah in the Patriarchal Era of its celebrated ancestors, Abraham, Isaac, and Jacob. The *Book of Genesis* tells the story of how God's providence brought Jacob and his family to the land of Egypt where their descendants were eventually enslaved for ten generations. Jacob was the inheritor of YHWH's promises to his grandfather Abraham and his father Isaac. Many years before the time of Jacob, YHWH told Abraham that the Egyptian enslavement of his progeny would last 400 years, but then he would bring about a great purpose through them. In the tenth generation, according to his word, YHWH accomplished a miraculous deliverance from the Egyptians through Moses. This momentous event, commonly known as the *Exodus*, is one of the great literary pillars upon which the entire Bible rests. They left Egypt as 12 tribes (named according to the 12 sons of Jacob), and God gave them his law at Mount Sinai as the basis for their new national identity and relationship to himself. They were no longer slaves but called to be a *kingdom of priests and a holy nation* unto YHWH, bearing his testimony in the world:

> "You yourselves have seen what I did to the Egyptians, and how I bore you on eagles' wings, and brought you to Myself. Now then, if you will indeed obey My voice and keep My covenant, then you shall be My own possession among all the peoples, for all the earth is Mine; and you shall be to Me a kingdom of priests and a holy nation. These are the words that you shall speak to the sons of Israel" (Exodus 19:4-6).

After testing them in the wilderness for 40 years, God used Joshua, the servant of Moses, to bring them into Canaan, the land of their inheritance as promised to the patriarchs. There, he established them as a tribal league (or federation) - a system of government by elders representing each of the 12 tribes. YHWH, who was their only king, called and anointed *charismatic* judges with the power of his Spirit to oversee the nation and deliver them in times of trouble. There was no central political machinery, royal privilege, or organized military. They were planted in Canaan to live as a society where YHWH dwelled and governed as described by Moses:

> "See, I have taught you statutes and judgments just as the LORD my God commanded me, that you should do thus in the land where you are entering to possess it. So keep and do them, for that is your wisdom and your understanding in the sight of the peoples who will hear all these statutes and say, 'Surely this great nation is a wise and understanding people'" (Deuteronomy 4:5-6).

The God-ordained dynamics of this social order were to demonstrate before the nations how a human community can thrive in harmony and well-being under the government of their creator. Israel was planted to establish not only a center of *perpetual priestly worship* in the temple, but also to live as a *societal expression* of God's heavenly kingdom on earth through holy living, civic justice, order, and harmony under his covenant.

GIVE US A KING!

In spite of all God had done for them, Israel remained a disobedient people throughout this era of rule by judges, which was characterized by repeated cycles of disobedience and deliverance. Yet, for reasons known only to God, he was pleased to be their exclusive king. Then, several hundred years after the Exodus, and as a result of a number of convergent factors, a crucial turning point in the history of the nation occurred. *First*, during the judicial term of Samuel the prophet, and consequently the last judge, Israel became fearful of the opposing threat of a well-organized, Philistine military force. *Second*, they knew that Samuel's disobedient sons did not have the same favor with God as their father had enjoyed. *Third*, they wrongly assumed that Samuel's sons would succeed him as judges in Israel, disregarding the fact that God had repeatedly used *charismatic anointing* by his Spirit as opposed to a royal blood-line to appoint his national leaders. As a result, the nation collectively rejected the tribal federation, demanding that YHWH give them a king:

> Then all the elders of Israel gathered together and came to Samuel at Ramah; and they said to him, "Behold, you have grown old, and your sons do not walk in your ways. Now appoint a king for us to judge us like all the nations." But the thing was displeasing in the sight of Samuel when they said, "Give us a king to judge us." And Samuel prayed to the LORD. The LORD said to Samuel, "Listen to the voice of the people in regard to all that they say to you, for they have not rejected you, but they have rejected Me from being king over them" (1 Samuel 8:4-7).

God gave them a king, and while he didn't allow this event to alter his redemptive purpose, it is clear that it was never his desire for his people. It was a role he had reserved for their Messiah at the proper time. He also told them that, as result of this choice, there would be numerous undesirable outcomes that Israel would regret. This collective manifestation of fear and unbelief is the *second* major illustration in the history of the nation of how ill-conceived choices have a way of creating their own inertia, resulting in consequences that had not been considered! The *first* example was the tragic failure at Kadesh-Barnea, where shortly after the Exodus, Israel fearfully halted at the entrance of the Promised Land because of the spies' report of the presence of giants. God's judgment for this action was to forbid them from entering the land, and they wandered for 40 years in the wilderness until the entire adult generation who left Egypt died (Numbers 13:25-14:24). It is significant that both of these events were motivated by fear and a lack of trust in God in the face of enemy powers.

THE SIGNIFICANCE OF THE TRANSITION
TO MONARCHY

In his book, *The Prophetic Imagination*, Walter Brueggemann insightfully expounds on the character of the transition from tribal league to monarchy (Brueggemann 2001:23-24). It was a movement from what he calls the *prophetic consciousness*, which characterized the time of Moses and the subsequent judges, to a *royal consciousness* that emerged during the reign of Solomon. This transition as described by Brueggemann is highly relevant to our understanding of Zechariah's visions. The prophetic consciousness under which the nation operated prior to the era of the monarchy was characterized by simple dependence on the direct intervention of God in the affairs of the nation. It was to bear not even the slightest resemblance to systems of imperial power such as Egypt:

> The participants in the Exodus found themselves, undoubtedly surprising to them, involved in the intentional formation of a *new social community* to match the vision of *God's freedom*. That new social reality, which is utterly discontinuous with Egypt, lasted in its alternative way for 250 years (Brueggemann 2001:7).

Even after the era of Israel's greatest leaders - Moses, and subsequently Joshua - the system proved to be workable in the first chapter of the Book of Judges, as all the heads of Israel came together to inquire of YHWH:

> Now it came about after the death of Joshua that the sons of Israel inquired of the LORD, saying, "Who shall go up first for us against the Canaanites, to fight against them?" The LORD said, "Judah shall go up; behold, I have given the land into his hand" (Judges 1:1-2).

Here, the reader is shown that the heads of the clans of Israel inquired, and God responded with definitive direction, resulting in a favorable outcome for the nation. However, from the end of Samuel's time onward, this direct kingship of God himself was replaced by a system with an Israelite king. This new order had all of the political trappings of built-in military protection, national financial security, foreign alliances, and a dependence on government intervention (to name a few). This was accompanied by a corpus of theological certitudes evidenced by the predominance of *proverbial wisdom*. Israel had grown weary of the God who was not predictable. Therefore, they were unwittingly prepared to embrace a system which could reduce him to (or replace him with) a collection of theological absolutes.

The proverbs became a perfect substitute. As important as the Proverbs are as guides to life (and they are), they should never be *absolutized* to the extent that God can be reduced to a predictable system of cause-and-effect. This misunderstanding and misuse of proverbial wisdom was the painful lesson learned by Job's counselor-friends. Job was a *righteous* man, but not a *perfect* man. Anyone reading his story can see the hint of *arrogance* in his character. His friends, rooted in proverbial wisdom, assumed a direct *causative* relationship between his pride and God's immediate judgment. However, we are clearly told in the first chapter of Job that his trial was *not because of his pride, but because of his righteousness*:

> There was a man in the land of Uz whose name was Job; and that man was blameless, upright, fearing God and turning away from evil... The LORD said to Satan, "Have you considered My servant Job? For there is no one like him on the earth, a blameless and upright man, fearing God and turning away from evil." Then Satan answered the LORD, "Does Job fear God for nothing? Have You not made a hedge about him and his house and all that he has, on every side? You have blessed the work of his hands, and his possessions have increased in the land. But put forth Your hand now and touch all that he has; he will surely curse You to Your face" (Job 1:1, 8-11).

Job's friends, like many of us, were unwittingly bound by their commitment to the royal consciousness, forced to assume that Job's dreadful circumstances could not possibly have been a consequence of *good behavior*. After all, the righteous are *blessed*, but the guilty *suffer*. That's what makes sense, and that is how God must behave and how we "domesticate" him - by keeping him under the control of our theological and reasoned out pre-commitments. We cannot have a God of freedom who allows the *righteous* to suffer. That violates our sensibilities and punches a hole in our iron-clad theology. God appropriately concludes the story with an affirmation that the friends of Job were misguided in their understanding, and Job who saw the sovereign God behind the contradiction - in spite of the venting of his frustration - was correct in his understanding:

> It came about after the LORD had spoken these words to Job, that the LORD said to Eliphaz the Temanite, "My wrath is kindled against you and against your two friends, because you have not spoken of Me what is right as My servant Job has. Now therefore, take for yourselves seven bulls and seven rams, and go to My servant Job, and offer up a burnt offering for yourselves, and My servant Job will pray for you. For I will accept him so that I may not do with you according to your folly, because you have not spoken of Me what is right, as My servant Job has" (Job 42:7-8).

The domestication of God thus became an unfortunate consequence of Solomon's regime and irreversibly upset the God-ordained balance of power in Israel. Under God's rule (the theocracy) there were limits to the amount of power concentrated in any one leader. Judges, tribal elders, and priests provided checks and balances on each other. This ensured that Israel's principal leaders never became corrupted by absolute power. The priests guarded the purity of the nation with respect to the temple rituals and holiness standards contained the law of Moses. The local elders and judges dealt with matters of civic justice which were also a part of the Mosaic corpus. The transition to monarchy resulted in the priesthood, who represented the transcendent *otherness* and *holiness* of God, no longer standing as a balancing tension *adjacent to the* state, but being relegated to a *subservient* role entirely in support of the state's objectives. The royal domestication of God had now extended beyond the theological realm into the political realm under the power of the king. The state, not God, became the absolute and the ensurer of the well being of the nation. To ensure this well-being, the inevitable outcome was that the priesthood became the servants of the state's interests. This was a key development also emphasized by John Bright:

> In any case the temptation was insidiously present to place religion at the service of the state. That the king had power over the clergy is illustrated by the fact that when the veteran priest Abiathar was so ill-advised as to hew to the wrong political line (1 Kgs. 1:7, 25), he was summarily dismissed by Solomon (1 Kgs. 2:26-27). . .It was inevitable that as the years passed, the aims of the state and the aims of religion should tend ever more closely to coincide; the state supports the cult, and the cult in turn exists for the state (Bright 1953:42-43).

This concept is also developed in the book, *The Just King: Monarchial Judicial Authority in Ancient Israel*, explaining that these conditions continued to become progressively entrenched in the national political system:

> The progressive encroachment of monarchic judicial authority upon the priestly sphere of jurisdiction was virtually complete by the time of Jehoshaphat, whose reform made the priestly role in justice fully subordinate to that of the monarch (Whitelam 1979:45).

When the people demanded a king, God told Samuel to warn them that they were making a terrible mistake in asking for a hierarchical government. He warned the Israelites that human kings would engage in personal and financial oppression of the people (1 Samuel 8:14-18). Those warnings proved to be true for the remaining 500 years of their history until they were exiled to Babylon.

There is a *necessary and healthy uncertainty* of God's next move which is embedded in the prophetic consciousness. It reminds the community of faith that we serve a sovereign God of freedom who will never be domesticated or fully subjected to our narrow definitions. The royal consciousness seeks to do precisely that - to define and reduce him to a *sealed* collection of questions and answers devoid of new possibilities. The *present* state, organization, or system of thought becomes absolutized and under the control of its leadership. It should also be noted that it is not the *world*, but the *people of God* who are in view in the account in First Samuel. How fearful it is for many a leader of God's people to be *unable to answer a question or resolve an apparent contradiction*! How much better it is to provide *certitudes*, where we supply not only the answers, but all of the acceptable questions as well, assuring the flock that we have everything under control, and no unknowns will intrude upon our comfortable church experience.

In addition, instead of being a *kingdom of priests*, citizens were viewed in an entirely utilitarian manner – that is, how they could best serve the interests of the state. The people accepted this new arrangement, with its new standard of success - affluence and perceived security rather than godliness. God desired distinctiveness and a divine testimony in the community he had formed to reflect *his own* image, where equality, justice, and godliness are held in high esteem as a beacon to the nations. Instead, Israel chose what *paralleled* the pagan nations - nationalistic pride, consumption, self preservation, and a "god" who existed to serve human interests, especially those of the state. That image – *the image of the beast* - was one which the biblical prophets often used to describe the oppressive, self-serving, power-hungry pagan nations who oppress the people of God (see Daniel 7:16-17). Jeremiah would later cry out that Israel had "perverted the national character into a foreign thing" (Bright 1953:42-43):

"Yet I planted you a choice vine,
A completely faithful seed.
How then have you turned yourself before Me
Into the degenerate shoots of a foreign vine?" (Jeremiah 2:21).

Israel received what they had demanded of God and became *like all the nations*, foolishly assuming that they could alter the character of their national existence without affecting their worship of God and their testimony to his name. The seeds of death had now been planted in the nation. The significance of this will become more evident as Zechariah's visions relating to the redefinition of Israel's national identity is discussed in the next chapter. As a final point of emphasis to further stress the failure of the kings (as well as the *system* of monarchy), Isaiah, in a striking look into the future experience of the nation, prophesied their release from exile. Their return to the land would not be a return to *monarchy*, but a restoration of the simpler form of leadership by *judges* in the pre-monarchial era, even linking it to righteousness and faithfulness:

> Therefore the Lord GOD of hosts,
> The Mighty One of Israel, declares,
> "Ah, I will be relieved of My adversaries
> And avenge Myself on My foes.
> I will also turn My hand against you,
> And will smelt away your dross as with lye
> And will remove all your alloy.
> *Then I will restore your judges as at the first,*
> And your counselors as at the beginning;
> After that you will be called the city of righteousness,
> A faithful city" (Isaiah 1:24-26).

So the nation continued on, having departed from the design of God. Subsequently, his warning through Samuel (1 Samuel 8:11-22) was substantiated through the course of their history. After the death of David's son, King Solomon (who built the first great temple in Jerusalem), the nation split into a northern kingdom (10 tribes named *Israel* or *Ephraim*), with a capital in Samaria, and a southern kingdom (2 tribes named *Judah*), with a capital in Jerusalem. The biblical stories of the kings are replete with accounts of political infighting and competing to gain power. Idolatry and pagan practice continued throughout their history. The law was neglected, the temple profaned. God repeatedly warned them through the prophets (and it is a major theme of the Old Testament prophets), that the nation was on a course toward disinheritance. God kept warning them that he was going to bring a foreign nation to destroy the city, the temple, and dispossess the nation of the land he had given them. Israel, however, fed by false prophets, chose to engage in the illusion that this could not be so. God could never allow his holy house, holy city, or holy people to fall to the powers of pagan nations. After all, they were *the chosen* of YHWH. The nation refused to listen to the authentic prophets sent by God, and late in the eighth century B.C., the collapse became imminent, as the shadow of a monstrous Assyrian Empire loomed over them, waiting to descend upon the disobedient people of God.

EXILE AND BEYOND

The warnings of the prophets became reality as the Assyrian armies descended from the north, and in 722 B.C. they shattered the northern kingdom, displacing the inhabitants from their tribal inheritance in the land of Canaan. God spared Judah in the south, not allowing Jerusalem to be taken, but nonetheless severely weakened by the invasion. Isaiah described the state of the nation following the devastating attacks, seeing Jerusalem barely standing as a tottering shelter left to collapse after the harvest is over:

Your land is desolate,
Your cities are burned with fire,
Your fields--strangers are devouring them in your presence;
It is desolation, as overthrown by strangers.
The daughter of Zion is left like a shelter in a vineyard,
Like a watchman's hut in a cucumber field, like a besieged city.
Unless the LORD of hosts
Had left us a few survivors,
We would be like Sodom,
We would be like Gomorrah (Isaiah 1:7-9).

Babylon, the next world power, defeated Assyria a century later, and began military invasions in Canaan around 605 B.C. As a result, the process of capture and deportation of the southern kingdom began. Finally and decisively in 586 B.C., the armies of Nebuchadnezzar, king of Babylon, leveled the walls of Jerusalem and destroyed the temple. This tragic account is recorded in 2 Kings 25:1-30 and 2 Chronicles 36:5-21. The writer of Second Kings pays specific attention to the destruction of the two pillars that stood at the entrance of the temple. These pillars typically represented the *high priest* and the *king*. The breaking apart of these pillars was merely a symbol of what had already begun centuries earlier:

> And *the pillars of bronze that were in the house of the LORD*, and the stands and the bronze sea that were in the house of the LORD, the Chaldeans broke in pieces and carried the bronze to Babylon (2 Kings 25:13).

The inheritance of God's people was brought entirely to ruin, and only a few poor were allowed to remain in Judea to tend the land.

THE RISE OF THE PERSIAN EMPIRE

Fifty years after that tragic event, God raised up the Persian Empire to defeat Babylon. Persia's king, Cyrus, decreed that the Jews should be allowed to go back and rebuild their temple and the city of Jerusalem:

> Now in the first year of Cyrus king of Persia, in order to fulfill the word of the LORD by the mouth of Jeremiah, the LORD stirred up the spirit of Cyrus king of Persia, so that he sent a proclamation throughout all his kingdom, and also put it in writing, saying: "Thus says Cyrus king of Persia, 'The LORD, the God of heaven, has given me all the kingdoms of the earth and He has appointed me to build Him a house in Jerusalem, which is in Judah.' Whoever there is among

you of all His people, may his God be with him! Let him go up to
Jerusalem which is in Judah and rebuild the house of the LORD, the
God of Israel; He is the God who is in Jerusalem" (Ezra 1:1-3).

In response to the decree, more than 43,000 Jews and several
thousand of their servants returned to the homeland, and a portion
of them went to Jerusalem to rebuild. The vast majority remained in
Babylon or fled to other parts of the world. Great joy and anticipa-
tion accompanied the rebuilding of the temple's new foundation as
described in Ezra 3:10-11, however, it wasn't long before opposition
arose from the surrounding peoples, and the rebuilding process came
to a halt. Fear had again crippled the people of God, keeping them
from completing the mission that YHWH had ordained for them.
Once more, a prophetic silence fell over the faltering and uncertain
remnant of God.

ZECHARIAH'S CONTEXT

Almost 20 years had passed since a humbled and tentative, yet
optimistic people of God had returned to rebuild but subsequently
abandoned the work. However, there was yet to be a restoration, the
significance of which Israel herself did not even fully seem to grasp at
that time:

Speak now to Zerubbabel the son of Shealtiel, governor of Judah,
and to Joshua the son of Jehozadak, the high priest, and to the remnant of the people saying, "Who is left among you who saw this
temple in its former glory? And how do you see it now? Does it
not seem to you like nothing in comparison? . . . *The latter glory of
this house will be greater than the former*," says the LORD of hosts,
"and in this place I will give peace," declares the LORD of hosts
(Haggai 2:2-3, 9).

The post-exilic world was a whole new experience for the nation.
There had been great promises offered by the former prophets. The

mountain of God was to be reestablished under Messiah's reign, with Israel as the head of nations, or so it was understood:

> The word which Isaiah the son of Amoz saw concerning
> Judah and Jerusalem.
> Now it will come about that in the last days the mountain of the
> house of the LORD
> Will be established as the chief of the mountains,
> And will be raised above the hills;
> And all the nations will stream to it.
> And many peoples will come and say,
> "Come, let us go up to the mountain of the LORD,
> To the house of the God of Jacob;
> That He may teach us concerning His ways
> And that we may walk in His paths."
> For the law will go forth from Zion
> And the word of the LORD from Jerusalem (Isaiah 2:1-3).

The glory would exceed even the Exodus from Egypt in the days of Moses:

> "Therefore behold, days are coming," declares the LORD, "when it will no longer be said, As the LORD lives, who brought up the sons of Israel out of the land of Egypt, but, 'As the LORD lives, *who brought up the sons of Israel from the land of the north and from all the countries where He had banished them.'* For I will restore them to their own land which I gave to their fathers" (Jeremiah 16:14-15).

The mountains and hills would shout for joy and the trees of the field would clap their hands exuberantly at the sight of the returning remnant of the people of God:

> "For you will go out with joy
> And be led forth with peace;
> The mountains and the hills will break forth into shouts of joy
> before you,
> And all the trees of the field will clap their hands" (Isaiah 55:12).

These are but a few of the great hopes of the nation that were anticipated in their release from exile. But these expectations, at least Israel's perception of them, had not materialized. Cyrus, who released the Jews after his defeat of Babylon, although benevolent, was a pagan foreigner - not a son of David - and therefore an unlikely Messiah. The temple and the city lie in shambles because the building process had ceased in the face of enemy opposition. From a human perspective, the promises of the former prophets who predicted a great restoration appeared to have failed miserably. The whole nation fell into a state of apathy and spiritual indifference concerning the things of God. The inevitable outcome was that they retreated from the work to focus on rebuilding and preserving their own private lives. The entire prophecy of the book of Malachi, which some have suggested may have been written by Zechariah (see Peterson 1995:3), addressed this spiritual in-difference of a people whose expectations had been dashed. In fact, each of the post-exilic prophets (Haggai, Zechariah, and Malachi) ad-dresses this apathetical attitude of their audiences.

Many years had passed and hopes had faded since that historic de-cree of King Cyrus. The long three-month journey back to Jerusalem to rebuild and restore was merely a faded memory. However, God had not forgotten. Suddenly the nation was awakened by the voice of the prophet Haggai:

> "Is it time for you yourselves to dwell in your paneled houses while this house lies desolate? Now therefore," thus says the LORD of hosts, "Consider your ways! You have sown much, but harvest little; you eat, but there is not enough to be satisfied; you drink, but there is not enough to become drunk; you put on clothing, but no one is warm enough; and he who earns, earns wages to put into a purse with holes." Thus says the LORD of hosts, "Consider your ways! Go up to the mountains, bring wood and rebuild the temple, that I may be pleased with it and be glorified," says the LORD (Haggai 1:4-8).

Not very accommodating was this fellow, Haggai. He didn't have time to engage their pain or disillusionment. The people of God had a mission to accomplish. He had arranged long ago, by the mouth of Isaiah, for their release from Babylon to fulfill his purpose:

> "It is I who says of Cyrus, 'he is my shepherd!
> And he will perform all my desire.'
> And he declares of Jerusalem, 'she will be built,'
> And of the temple, 'your foundation will be laid'" (Isaiah 44:28).

There was an encounter with divine destiny on the horizon. The people responded to the exhortations of the prophet, and Haggai was soon joined by another, a young priest named Zechariah. Together they took their place before the people of God and prophesied to encourage the rebuilding process.

RETURN TO YHWH OF HOSTS!

Zechariah's *Prologue* (Zechariah 1:1-6) indicates that at the time of his visions, Darius was the king of Persia and the most powerful ruler in the ancient east. The Jews, although free to return to their homeland, remained under Persian rule. In Zechariah's time, the restored people of God had long since set down their building tools in fear and disillusionment. They had encountered forces that did not want God's throne to be reestablished. Resistance and conflict arose. Some gave up, tired of the battle, unable to fight and build at the same time – much like us – holding tools in one hand while carrying a sword in the other (cf. Nehemiah 4:18). It is completely understandable that the community would eventually become disheartened and disillusioned.

It is for this very important reason that in Zechariah 1:3-4, God identifies himself as the LORD (YHWH) of *Hosts* (or *Armies*). In Hebrew, *YHWH Sabaoth* is a significant name in post-exilic literature, appearing 91 times in Haggai, Zechariah, and Malachi. YHWH is his covenant name, which is derived from the Hebrew word *hayah: to be*. As YHWH of Hosts, he was calling back to memory ancient prophets like Isaiah and Jeremiah who spoke prior to the exile. He was reminding the nation that *it was God* who sent the Babylonians to disestablish Israel and Judah. *It was also God* who controlled the powers of heaven and earth at that moment in their history. He, as *the self-existent, future-generating God* was affirming his faithfulness and ability to protect and nurture their weakened and relatively insignificant post-exilic community. The declaration of this particular name, more than any other in the Old Testament, attested to Israel that their covenant-keeping God had not forgotten them and was in absolute control of all forces seen and unseen. In these introductory statements, the Lord was saying in effect, "Turn from your sin, unbelief, and disillusionment. Those are the things that have eroded the strength of the nation since the beginning. I told you beforehand what was going to happen, and I spoke through my prophets, and it happened. Now, I am speaking to you again. My words have proven to be reliable. You can trust my words."

But why did the Lord call this fragile remnant which had suffered such immense conflict and disillusionment to *repentance*? One would think He might have something more *therapeutic* available for them at a time like this. What God saw, and what the returnees needed to understand, was that although they had come back to their *homeland* and the promise of their inheritance, they had not returned to faith in *YHWH himself*. Their relationship with him had to be right before he could unlock the door to their future. Therefore, the comfort must wait. God never affirms his people in their unbelief and disobedience:

> And without faith it is impossible to please Him, for he who comes to God must believe that He is and that He is a rewarder of those who seek Him (Hebrews 11:6).

It takes only a little bit of interpretive imagination seasoned with insight into human nature to see what had occurred, and it is certainly worthy of attention. The disillusionment that accompanied the failure of the rebuilding process led the people of God down a highly predictable path. *Disillusionment* is a common human reaction to *failed expectations*, accompanied by a *loss of prophetic vision* (what we anticipate).

This loss of vision then becomes a breeding ground for *apathy or spiritual indifference* because it is the sense of purpose that sparks our motivation to discipline, structure, and restraint. When the vision is strong, we value restraints because they are seen as vital to achieving the vision. It is much like an athlete training to compete for the prize, as Paul told the Corinthians:

> Do you not know that those who run in a race all run, but only one receives the prize? Run in such a way that you may win. Everyone who competes in the games *exercises self-control in all things. They then do it to receive a perishable wreath, but we an imperishable.* Therefore I run in such a way, as not without aim; I box in such a way, as not beating the air; but I discipline my body and make it my slave, so that, after I have preached to others, I myself will not be disqualified (1 Corinthians 9:24-27).

When vision has failed or becomes blurred, the human tendency is to cast off those restraints, no longer valuing or feeling the need for them. This is what is behind the great proverb:

> Where there is no vision, the people are unrestrained. . . (Proverbs 29:18a – note: The KJV uses "*perish*" in place of NASB's "*unrestrained.*" Other later translations NIV, CEV, ESV, LITV, and NLT also have translated the original Hebrew as meaning *to lack restraint*).

Malachi sees the same symptoms of apathy as he responds to Israel's complaint:

> "Your words have been arrogant against Me," says the LORD. "Yet you say, 'What have we spoken against You?' You have said, 'It is vain to serve God; and *what profit is it that we have kept His charge, and that we have walked in mourning* before the LORD of hosts?'" (Malachi 3:13-14).

The perceived failure of God to fulfill the earlier promises led Israel to the conclusion that their devotion was of no real value.

Eventually, small compromises gave way to greater sins. It is commonly understood by commentators that this was the state of the nation at that time in their history - that is, a disillusioned people whose expectations never fully materialized. Given that, it was necessary for God to call their attention to the outcome of their unbelief before he could comfort and re-energize their hope. Although Zechariah 1:6 is open to interpretation, it would appear that the people of God responded to Zechariah's call to repentance. Effectively, that meant they acknowledged they were not *victims* but in fact, had been *judged* by God for their centuries of unfaithfulness. In other words, they demonstrated a willingness to agree with God's perspective and assessment of both their historical and present situation. This acknowledgment was all that was needed to prepare their hearts to receive the prophet's fresh vision:

> On the twenty-fourth day of the eleventh month, which is the month Shebat, in the second year of Darius, the word of the LORD came to Zechariah the prophet, the son of Berechiah, the son of Iddo, as follows: (Zechariah 1:7).

In this opening chapter, we learn that God was about to take Zechariah on a journey through a series of night visions. There were to be eight in all. They constitute the first six chapters of the book, and through them God was showing to his prophet the divine purpose behind His people's present experience. Zechariah was going to see things that would help the community of faith through their *crisis of reorientation* and see more clearly the universal purpose of God. Furthermore, the constructs which God had in mind were not reminiscent of the past, but a forging ahead to new possibilities for the present and the future of his people. Before we individually examine each of the visions, however, it will be useful see God's remarkable design in this encounter with his prophet because the eight visions, as recorded, form a literary masterpiece. There is both a *literary pattern* embedded in the messages conveyed in the visions, as well as a distinguishable pattern of *geographical movement*.

STRUCTURE IN ZECHARIAH 1-6

The prophet's visionary experiences appear to follow both *thematic* and *geographical* patterns. These eight visions seen by Zechariah are in the form of what is called a "chiasm" (pronounced *ky-asm*). A chiasm is often expressed graphically as one-half of the Greek letter "chi" (which looks very similar to a cursive "X"). Chiasm (or chiasmus) is a literary device not uncommon to the ancient world and quite frequently found in the Bible. Words or themes in a chiasm move in a line by line sequence (shown as A, B, C, etc. in the examples to follow) from a starting point, toward a *central theme* or *transition*. From the central point(s) the words or themes retrace their steps (in reverse order, shown as C', B', A', etc.) back to the starting point. The idea in A matches the idea in A', B matches the idea in B', and so on.

LITERARY STRUCTURE

To illustrate, below is a simple chiasm found in Genesis 9:6 where, speaking to Noah, God invests man with the power of self-government. Notice how the first and last key words match, as do the second and second to last, then the two center elements (sometimes only *one*) form the central theme that *man* is being empowered by God to execute justice:

GENESIS 9:6A

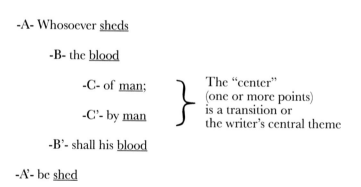

-A- Whosoever <u>sheds</u>

    -B- the <u>blood</u>

        -C- of <u>man;</u>   The "center"
(one or more points)
is a transition or
the writer's central theme

        -C'- by <u>man</u>

    -B'- shall his <u>blood</u>

-A'- be <u>shed</u>

Figure 1.1

The structure of the entire *Book of Revelation* may be seen as a chiasm. Below is just one of many variations, indicating that worship is the central theme of the book.

A STRUCTURE OF THE BOOK OF REVELATION:

-A-Prologue: Alpha and Omega   1:1-8

  -B-Seven Churches   1:9-3:22

    -C-Sealing the Saints   4:1-8:5

      -D-Warning of Judgment   8:2, 6 -11:19

        -E-Conflict over Worship   12:1-14:20

      -D'-Execution of Judgment   15:1-18:24

    -C'-Sealing of the Wicked   19:1-20:15

  -B'-Victorious Church   21:1-22:5

-A'-Epilogue: Alpha and Omega   22:6-21

Figure 1.2

Regarding Zechariah, as is often the case there is more than one opinion, even regarding the number of visions. However, most commentators agree that Zechariah 1-6 seems to follow a chiastic structure. Below, similar to some, is my own interpretation (note: the center is an oracle rather than a visionary image):

ZECHARIAH 1 – 6:

-A- Judgment (Israel Humbled)   1:7-17

  -B- Builders (Carpenters)   1:18-21

    -C- City (Enlarged – Redefined)   2:1-13

      -D- Cleansing Grace (Joshua)   3:1-7

        -E- "My Servant the Branch"   3:8-10

      -D'- Empowering Grace (Zerubbabel)   4:1-14

    -C'- Flying Scroll (Cities Purged)   5:1-4

  -B'- Woman & Ephah (Building)   5: 5-11

-A'- Judgment (Babylon Humbled)   6:1-8

Figure 1.3

GEOGRAPHICAL MOVEMENT

Beyond the literary structure of the visions is the remarkable pattern of the *geographic locations* of the visions. The chiastic structure is not only literary, but appears to be geographical. The eight visions allowed Zechariah to see God at work in the surrounding nations, where God assures and promises his people that his domain (the city and the temple) will be restored and builders will be raised up. Moving to the land of Israel and the city of Jerusalem (these are referred to as the *covenant realm* or *domain*); God declares his vision for a newly reconstituted and inclusive city. Next, in the inner sanctuary of the temple, the necessary transition from sin to grace is observed as the high priest stands as proxy for the remnant's transformation from a filth covered body to a body of light shining seven times its former brightness. All of this comes as a result of the grace of God – a grace and purpose that will be fully disclosed in one yet come, called *the Branch*. From there our prophet journeyed back out in reverse sequence, where again, in the covenant realm, internal and external hindrances among the people of God that pollute his testimony are identified and purged. Finally, when his work is completed in his own domain, Zechariah observes as God turns his attention to bringing judgment upon the oppressors of his people.

The following diagram (in chiasmic structure) illustrates that the geographical movement in Zechariah's visionary experience, as described above, does not correspond on a one-to-one basis with the visions. The first two visions seem to occur in the regions outside of Jerusalem and the land. The third vision is in the city itself. The sanctuary location involves two visions, one in the Holy of Holies, and one in the Holy Place of the temple. Between these two visions is the oracle concerning the Branch. Two visions are then seen back again in the vicinity of Jerusalem and the land, and the final vision includes the regions outside of the covenant realm.

GEOGRAPHICAL MOVEMENT
ZECHARIAH 1 – 6:

-A-The Nations	1:7-21	
-B- The Covenant Realm	2:1-13	
-C- The Temple Proper		3:1-4:14
-B'- The Covenant Realm	5:1-11	
-A'- The Nations	6:1-8	

Figure 1.4

THE SIGNIFICANCE OF THE LITERARY STRUCTURE

The preceding seeks to emphasize the significance of the literary structure of these visions. Infinitely more than a mere academic exercise, the sequence, themes, and locations of Zechariah's visionary journey were uniquely designed by God to unfold a progressive message to his people. The literary composition strengthens the content, creating a single context - a unified whole, allowing us not only to read, but also to *participate* in Zechariah's journey. Recognizing this makes the study of this great book an engagement with a wonderfully crafted, divine design rather than a disjointed collection of mysterious metaphors.

Chapter 2

THE FIRST VISION
THE CEDAR HAS TO GO

Zechariah's first vision took him outside of Jerusalem to witness a report by God's messengers who had been out among *the nations* (notably the Persian Empire). There, he observed an intercessory plea for restoration and the ensuing response from YHWH. This provided the prophet with a divine perspective of Israel's situation. There are several notable elements of this vision that contribute to our theme of *redefinition and enlargement*. Zechariah observed a mounted messenger of the Lord, followed by three additional messengers among a grove of myrtle trees in a ravine. The mounted messengers had been sent by God to patrol the earth and had observed that all was peaceful and quiet. The theme of this vision is God's judgment, which humbled and redefined the national character of his people through the process of exile.

> I saw at night, and behold, a man was riding on a red horse, and he was standing among the myrtle trees, which were in the ravine, with red, sorrel and white horses behind him. Then I said, "My lord, what are these?" And the angel who was speaking with me said to me, "I will show you what these are." And the man who was standing among the myrtle trees answered and said, "These are those whom the LORD has sent to patrol the earth." So they answered the angel of the LORD who was standing among the myrtle trees and said, "We have patrolled the earth, and behold, all the earth is peaceful and quiet" (Zechariah 1:8-11).

THE MYRTLE TREES

In former times, particularly during the era of the *monarchy*, the nation of Israel with its capital city of Jerusalem was often symbolized in the Bible as a great *cedar* tree. The pre-exilic cedar imagery is drawn from its extensive use in the construction of the temple and the king's palace.

> Then Hiram king of Tyre sent messengers to David with cedar trees and carpenters and stonemasons; and they built a house for David (2 Samuel 5:11).

> So he [Solomon] built the house [of God] and finished it; and he covered the house with beams and planks of cedar (1 Kings 6:9).

In Ezekiel 17, the prophet refers to Jerusalem as "Lebanon" because Lebanon is the region where cedars grow in abundance. In the following parable, the *top* of the cedar is Jeconiah, king of Judah, and the *young twigs* are his children, along with the leaders who were exiled to Babylon. The army of the Chaldeans is characterized by the *great eagle*, the land of Chaldea is *the land of merchants*, and its Chaldean capital city, Babylon, is seen as the *city of traders*.

> ...Thus says the Lord GOD, "A great eagle with great wings, long pinions and a full plumage of many colors came to Lebanon and took away the top of the cedar. He plucked off the topmost of its young twigs and brought it to a land of merchants; he set it in a city of traders" (Ezekiel 17:3-4).

In this reference to the *destruction of the temple* by Babylon, Zechariah's later description is that of a *cedar forest*, which has been felled to the ground and burned – an interpretation also found in the *Jerusalem Talmud*, which states:

Said Rabban Yohanan Ben Zakkai to the Temple, "O Temple, why do you frighten us? We know that you will end up destroyed. For it has been said, 'Open your doors, O Lebanon, that the fire may devour your cedars'" (Zechariah 11:1) (Sota 6:3 – quoted in Federoff 2005)

The full context of Zechariah 11:1-3 reads:

Open your doors, O Lebanon,
That a fire may feed on your cedars.
Wail, O cypress, for *the cedar has fallen,*
Because the glorious trees have been destroyed;
Wail, O oaks of Bashan,
For the *impenetrable forest* has come down.
There is a sound of the shepherds' wail, for their glory is ruined;
There is a sound of the young lions' roar,
For the pride of the Jordan is ruined (Zechariah 11:1-3).

The cedar is mentioned in the Old Testament only six times from Genesis to Second Samuel. This spans the entire history of the Bible up to the crowning of Israel's first king, Saul. After the dawning of the kingdom era in Second Samuel, the cedar is mentioned 40 times. It has a clear association with the beauty and stature of ancient Jerusalem, the temple, and the king's palace, which were so prominent during the era of the monarchy.

Now that the old paradigm, with its outward beauty had fallen, God offered a new symbol, a *redefinition* of Israel's national identity - the *myrtle*. Parenthetically, the myrtle metaphor is also found in the *Book of Esther,* which is set against the background of post-exilic Israel. Esther, herself is a *type* of the returning remnant. Esther was her Persian name, but her original Hebrew name was *Hadassah* (Esther 2:7), which comes from the Hebrew word *hadas* meaning *myrtle.* In Zechariah's first vision, the nation was characterized by a lowly grove of myrtle being watched over by a mounted messenger of the Lord and his entourage.

The myrtle was also foreseen by Isaiah the prophet, writing in a vision of Israel's return from Babylon:

> For you will go out with joy
> And be led forth with peace;
> The mountains and the hills will break forth into shouts of joy
> before you,
> And all the trees of the field will clap their hands.
> Instead of the thorn bush the cypress will come up,
> And *instead of the nettle the myrtle will come up,*
> And it will be a memorial to the LORD,
> For an everlasting sign which will not be cut off (Isaiah 55:12-13).

Behind all of this imagery is the message that *the cedar had to go and the myrtle had to grow.* The cedar represented all that was externally impressive and lofty. It is tall and majestic, having a highly visible branch structure. This symbolized Israel's *former existence* during the kingdom era. Like the cedar, Jerusalem and her temple were majestic and beautiful in their external adornment. The myrtle by contrast is lowly and relatively speaking, much less impressive. However, unlike the cedar, which only flourishes in restricted areas such as Syria, the myrtle is robust and capable of growing anywhere throughout the region. This is indicative of enlargement since, as a positive consequence of the exile, Israel's influence had already begun to expand universally. No longer "confined" to Canaan, but scattered throughout the world, they brought the knowledge of YHWH with them. This will be further discussed in the third vision. Additionally, a little research yields that the myrtle's small trunks often intertwine to form the trunk of a larger, stronger tree suggesting that it is connected *relationally* within the grove. This is in stark contrast to the singular, *independent*, majestic structure of the great cedar.

When God came looking for fruit and found none, he sent the Babylonian armies to bring down that which had not produced what he desired. Now, 50 years after the tragic fall of the city and the temple, and 70 years after the exile began, a lowly myrtle grove appears in a ravine, which speaks of a people in a vulnerable, humbled, and despairing place. In spite of their apparent vulnerability, the nation was now characterized by a symbol reflecting a new and robust nature. To further enhance the impact of this imagery, Meredith G. Kline has made a strong argument suggesting that the Hebrew word "*metsulah*" which is here translated *ravine*, should actually be translated *deep* or *depths*. Among his observations, he notes that it is the same word used in Exodus 15:5 to describe the *depths of the sea* into which Pharaoh's chariots were hurled (Kline 2001:6-7):

> The deeps cover them; they went down into the depths [*metsulah*] like a stone (Exodus 15:5).

In this vision, we are given an image of a new creation about to dawn. It is a common theme in biblical history when God begins something new. The Spirit first hovered over the *deep* at the dawn of creation. The children of Israel later stood at the banks of the Red Sea (*the deep*) as God prepared them to cross over as a new nation. Now, in a new national situation, Zechariah observed the familiar image of the people of God gathered by *the deep* as a prelude to yet another new and creative work of YHWH.

THE MOUNTED MESSENGERS

In spite of the tentative position in which the people of God found themselves, the mounted angelic messengers in this vision were standing among them. God had not abandoned his people, and the riders have been traversing throughout the land to assess the state of the world on his behalf. The colors of the horses immediately bring to mind the vision of John in chapter 6 of the *Book of Revelation*, where their colors are given the specific meanings - conquest, war, famine, and pestilence (Revelation 6:1-5). An interesting feature of Zechariah's vision, however, is that the white horse is positioned (or at least mentioned) *last* in contrast to his being the *leading* rider in two of John's visions. The White Horse Rider in Revelation 19 is clearly the Lord Jesus *leading* the hosts of the Lord (Revelation 19:11-17), and was arguably the *leading* rider in Revelation 6:2 as well, if one believes biblical symbolism is consistent. This suggests in Zechariah that the pre-incarnate Christ had positioned himself *behind* those messengers who administered his judgments. The Bible uses other metaphors to convey this same idea of God's purging judgments preceding his presence, besides those in Zechariah's vision. Note the words of the Psalmist, who sees *fire* going before the Lord:

> Out of Zion, the perfection of beauty, God has shone forth. May our God come and not keep silence; *Fire devours before Him,* and it is very tempestuous around Him (Psalm 50:2-3).

The prophets see a messenger of the Lord clearing the way before his presence:

> "Behold, I am going to send *My messenger,* and *he will clear the way before Me.* And the Lord, whom you seek, will suddenly come to His temple; and the messenger of the covenant, in whom you delight, behold, He is coming," says the LORD of hosts. "But who can endure the day of His coming? And who can stand when He appears? For *He is like a refiner's fire* and like fullers' soap" (Malachi 3:1-2).

> A voice is calling,
> "Clear the way for the LORD in the wilderness;
> Make smooth in the desert a highway for our God.
> Let every valley be lifted up,
> And every mountain and hill be made low;
> And let the rough ground become a plain,
> And the rugged terrain a broad valley;
> Then the glory of the LORD will be revealed,
> And all flesh will see it together;
> For the mouth of the LORD has spoken" (Isaiah 40:3-5).

These texts indicate that he is *behind* the fire. There is a cleansing, purging fire, representative of judgment that precedes the arrival of God into the human situation. What goes before him purges all that is unholy and calls His people to repentance, making them ready for his presence. Now, although the people of God had experienced a season of fierce judgments, they needed to understand that they were not victims of the random aggression of a foreign nation but were, in fact, subjects of YHWH's purifying chastisements that precede his presence. The trailing *White Horse Rider* was arriving on the scene on the heels of those purging messengers sent before him. They were then sent out to observe and report back regarding the state of matters on the earth. God, the mounted Messiah, was arriving to preserve his people from their enemies and lead them in rebuilding.

THE WORLD AT REST

The Lord's patrol reported back that the world was enjoying un-precedented peace and rest under the reign of the Persian king, Darius (v. 11), while God's people remained in their weakened and tentative state. The messenger of the Lord then inquired regarding this strange state of affairs:

> I saw at night, and behold, a man was riding on a red horse, and he was standing among the myrtle trees which were in the ravine, with red, sorrel and white horses behind him. Then I said, "My lord, what are these?" And the angel who was speaking with me said to me, "I will show you what these are." And the man who was standing among the myrtle trees answered and said, Then the angel of the LORD said, "O LORD of hosts, how long will You have no compassion for Jerusalem and the cities of Judah, with which You have been indignant these seventy years?" The LORD answered the angel who was speaking with me with gracious words, comforting words. So the angel who was speaking with me said to me, "Proclaim, saying, 'Thus says the LORD of hosts, I am exceedingly jealous for

Jerusalem and Zion. But I am very angry with the nations who are at ease; for while I was only a little angry, they furthered the disaster. Therefore thus says the LORD, "I will return to Jerusalem with compassion; My house will be built in it," declares the LORD of hosts, "and a measuring line will be stretched over Jerusalem. Again, proclaim, saying, 'Thus says the LORD of hosts, "My cities will again overflow with prosperity, and the LORD will again comfort Zion and again choose Jerusalem"'" (Zechariah 1:12-17).

This discourse between the angel and **YHWH** is actually quite remarkable. Our text indicates there was a season of unprecedented peace and stability in the world, possibly (though disputed by some) as a result of Persian rule under Darius. How much energy is expended in the world, seeking to achieve the goal of world peace as if it were a divine objective! That is not to suggest that world peace in and of itself is necessarily a bad thing. However, the nations were at peace and *God was not pleased.* This suggests that the world, no matter what degree of peace and safety it may achieve, cannot be right when God's house lies desolate leaving no testimony to him in the earth. Of course, the princes of this world *are at rest* when the voice of the people of God has been silenced. However, it is quite a different story when God's throne is established. To this point we observe the words of the second Psalm:

Why are the *nations in an uproar* and the peoples devising a vain thing? The kings of the earth take their stand And the rulers take counsel together Against the LORD and against His Anointed, saying, "Let us tear their fetters apart And cast away their cords from us!" ... But as for Me, *I have installed My King upon Zion, My holy mountain.* I will surely tell of the decree of the LORD: He said to Me, "You are My Son, Today I have begotten You. Ask of Me, and I will surely give the nations as Your inheritance, and the very ends of the earth as Your possession." ... Now therefore, O kings, show discernment; Take warning, O judges of the earth. Worship the LORD with reverence and rejoice with trembling. Do homage to the Son, that He not become angry, and you perish in the way, for His wrath may soon be kindled. How blessed are all who take refuge in Him! (Psalm 2:1-3; 6-8; 10-12).

When God's throne is established among his people, the nations roar in defiance against his restraints on the wickedness of men. Christ's lordship and testimony expose the true condition of the world, calling it to repentance. The nations were only at rest under Persian rule because God's people (the place of his dominion) were in ruin, so there was no reason for the ungodly principalities to rear up in rage. They presumed themselves to be in an unchallenged position of control. This was vividly exemplified on the day that Jesus was cruci-fied. Undoubtedly under the assumption that they were finally ridding themselves of a troublesome rabbi, Herod and Pilate, who were long standing political *enemies*, suddenly and mysteriously became "friends":

And Herod with his soldiers, after treating Him [Jesus] with con-tempt and mocking Him, dressed Him in a gorgeous robe and sent Him back to Pilate. Now *Herod and Pilate became friends with one another that very day*, for before they had been enemies with each other (Luke 23:11-12).

The Persian Empire's illusion of control was about to be *crushed*. The first vision concludes with God's response to the intercession of the angel as one of assurance and compassion for his people. However, this assurance did not come until the people of God repented. Once that was accomplished, his attention turned to the forces he allowed to bring down the pride of Israel leaving his people lowly, broken, and uncertain. These powers became the object of his anger because their mistreatment of the nation went beyond what he had authorized, and they were now arrogantly indifferent to the plight of his people. YHWH gave assurance that he is jealous over his people and his tes-timony and would indeed reestablish his house and his city. He would then bring vengeance upon his enemies and demonstrate to them and his own people that YHWH is the indisputable Lord of *all* the earth.

CONTEMPORARY RELEVANCE

A redefined people of God are those rooted in repentance, genuine humility, and an unwavering trust in God when faced with uncertainty and vulnerability. They also demonstrate the capacity to flourish in challenging, unfamiliar and less than optimum conditions and environments.

1. The *Prologue* teaches us that repentance is an inescapable prelude to any fresh revelation of God. Whatever our circumstances, we cannot afford the luxury of seeing ourselves as victims, nor allow failed expectations to take us down the road to spiritual indifference and compromise. A fundamental mistake which most often leads to these conditions is to misinterpret what God has promised. When *unreal* expectations are shattered, we don't question whether the expectations were faulty; we question God who didn't fulfill them. How often these self-centered expectations fail us - leaving a trail of hurt and disillusionment. As our text suggests, God's response is not merely *commiseration or condolences* but a call to repentance and a realignment of our goals and desires to those of the kingdom.

2. The *cedar-myrtle* imagery suggests that we must be broken from our tendency to desire that which is impressive to man. Core value systems derived from cultural conditioning that remain so deeply ingrained in the life of the believer bring with them standards of success and impressiveness that have no place in the kingdom of God. That which represents God in the world must bear his image and not that of an earthly counterfeit. God has chosen the weak to confound the strong, the foolish to confound the wise, and the poor to inherit the kingdom. In spite of this, we repeatedly choose that which is esteemed by men, but not God.

3. Akin to number 2, the *cedar-myrtle* also suggests that what is capable of growth only in narrow, optimum conditions (the cedar) must give way to that which is robust and capable of growth in any conditions (the myrtle). This means, for example, that we cannot cloister ourselves from the harsh realities of the violence and poverty of our urban communities. Growth in compassion and the ability to associate and engage those whose environment is radically different from our own is a foundation of our faith. It has been a tragic departure from the faith in the United States over the past 50 years that our neighborhood churches have packed up and left urban and other needy neighborhoods to follow the movement of their tithing membership to safer, wealthier suburban locations. Following Solomon's *royal consciousness*, we have opted for convenience and financial security rather than planting and investing ourselves in the locality of our mission to those who are in need, and to whom we have been called:

> The Spirit of the Lord is upon me,
> Because He *anointed me to preach the gospel to the poor.*
> He has sent me to proclaim release to the captives,
> And recovery of sight to the blind,
> To set free those who are oppressed,
> To proclaim the favorable year of the Lord (Luke 4:18-19).

> And turning His gaze toward His disciples, He began to say, "Blessed are you who are poor, for yours is the kingdom of God. Blessed are you who hunger now, for you shall be satisfied. Blessed are you who weep now, for you shall laugh" (Luke 6:20-21).

The *gospel to the poor* is inseparably integrated into the message of Jesus and by extension, his commission to the Church. The Church is not the Church if it has no *direct* interaction with the poor. The gospel of Jesus Christ is repeatedly emphasized in the New Testament as *good news to the poor* and the certainty of an eschatological reversal in the age to come that will bring down the privileged and exalt those who have no power base in this life. A redefined and enlarged people of God are capable of relationships and growth in any setting that they find themselves. They are capable of authentic relationships because their identity is no longer in their pre-Christian socio-economic reality, but "hid with Christ in God" (Colossians 3:3) – *along with* all those who are called by his name, regardless of natural heritage or socio-economic status. They are capable of growth inasmuch as redefinition *precedes* enlargement, and God is able to use them in places not before possible.

4. The *messenger-horsemen* remind us that our Sovereign God, although not always distinguishable in the forefront of our circumstances, is always there as the *White Horse Rider*, ready to protect and deliver his people. Eugene Merrill writes:

> ...the mission of the four horses and their riders (or at least the rider of one of them, the red horse) was to walk about on the whole earth (v. 10). The verb form here ... is extremely significant, for in that stem the verb frequently has the idea of dominion. To walk about on the earth is to assert sovereignty over it (Merrill: bible.org).

Although the aftermath of crisis may leave us tentative and vulnerable, he is ever and always scanning the larger picture, jealous over his testimony in the world and the well-being of his people. He is indeed, the omniscient God, knowing and seeing all. Not a detail of our lives, nor the conditions of the world around us escape his notice, for all things serve to fulfill his purpose in Christ through the Church.

Chapter 3

THE SECOND VISION
HORNS & CARPENTERS

The first vision quickly faded as the prophet's eyes lifted to focus on a new set of images. He saw four horns, which he was told by the angel had scattered the people of God. He then saw four craftsmen arriving to confront, terrify, and cast down the four horns.

> Then I lifted up my eyes and looked, and behold, there were four horns. So I said to the angel who was speaking with me, "What are these?" And he answered me, "These are the horns which have scattered Judah, Israel, and Jerusalem." Then the LORD showed me four craftsmen. I said, "What are these coming to do?" And he said, "These are the horns which have scattered Judah so that no man lifts up his head; but these craftsmen have come to terrify them, to throw down the horns of the nations who have lifted up their horns against the land of Judah in order to scatter it" (Zechariah 1:18-21).

THE FOUR HORNS

In the Bible, the number *four* symbolically represents something that is *total*, *universal*, or *multi-directional*, as observed in each of the following texts:

> For thus says the Lord GOD, "How much more when I send My four severe judgments against Jerusalem: sword, famine, wild beasts and plague to cut off man and beast from it!" (Ezekiel 14:21).

> After this I saw four angels standing at the four corners of the earth, holding back the four winds of the earth, so that no wind would blow on the earth or on the sea or on any tree (Revelation 7:1).

A *horn* is universally understood as a symbol of power, strength, or kingly authority. As one of many examples in the Bible, the prophet Daniel's vision of the approaching conflict between Medo-Persia and the Greek empire of Alexander the Great was interpreted by the angel Gabriel as follows:

> The ram which you saw with the two horns represents the kings of Media and Persia. The shaggy goat represents the kingdom of Greece, and *the large horn that is between his eyes is the first king. The broken horn and the four horns that arose in its place represent four kingdoms* which will arise from his nation, although not with his power (Daniel 8:20-22).

Daniel was informed that each horn in the vision represented a specific king of a specific kingdom. Greece, the shaggy goat with a large horn, is generally agreed to have been Alexander the Great. Since Alexander had no heir, the four horns that arose represented his four generals who, after his death, each took control of a portion of his empire. Zechariah's vision however, indicates that there were four *unnamed* horns that scattered God's people. Our first inclination is to attempt to assign names to the horns, such as Philistia, Assyria, Egypt, Babylon, or Persia which may certainly be implied by the events of history. While this is not out of the question, the fact that: 1) they are not specifically *named*, 2) they are not described as *kings*, and 3) they are not described as being attached to anything *living* affords the opportunity to engage in some interpretive imagination to see beyond the *political* realm of conflict and into the *spiritual* realm.

Horns of power typically served as symbolic ornamentation on the corners of both sacred and pagan altars. In Israel's sanctuary complexes (first the tabernacle and then the temple) horns were crafted onto the *brazen altar* in the court and the *altar of incense* within the Holy Place of the sanctuary:

Then he [Moses] made the *altar of burnt offering* of acacia wood, five cubits long, and five cubits wide, square, and three cubits high. He made its *horns on its four corners*, its horns being of one piece with it, and he overlaid it with bronze (Exodus 38:1-2).

Moreover, you shall make an *altar as a place for burning incense*; you shall make it of acacia wood. Its length shall be a cubit, and its width a cubit, it shall be square, and its height shall be two cubits; *its horns* shall be of one piece with it. You shall overlay it with pure gold, its top and its sides all around, and its horns; and you shall make a gold molding all around for it (Exodus 30:1-3).

Together, these two temple furnishings symbolized: 1) God's saving power for the people of his domain accomplished through the blood of sacrifice, and 2) access to his power through prayer and intercession. The sacrificial altar served as a replica of the land of Israel (the domain of YHWH), often described as having four corners, as spoken by the Lord to Ezekiel just prior to the destruction of Jerusalem in 586 B.C.:

And you, son of man, thus says the Lord GOD to the land of Israel, "An end! The end is coming on the *four corners* of the land" (Ezekiel 7:2).

The four horns, as symbols of power, were boundary markers surrounding and protecting the inhabitants of YHWH'S land, his testimony, and his capital city of Jerusalem. The horns ornamented the periphery of the brazen altar of sacrifice because the land of Israel was uniquely the place where atonement was made for sin through the sacrifices. It also foreshadowed the sacrifice of Lord Jesus, who would die for our sins in the Promised Land. The altar of incense was also horned, signifying that YHWH's domain (the land – again symbolized by the four cornered altar) was the place where priestly prayer and devotion to YHWH arose. The Old Testament symbolism of the incense of prayer was clarified in John's vision in the eighth chapter of the *Book of Revelation*:

Another angel came and stood at the altar, holding a golden censer; and much incense was given to him, so that *he might add it to the prayers of all the saints* on the golden altar which was before the throne. And the smoke of the incense, with the prayers of the saints, went up before God out of the angel's hand (Revelation 8:3-4).

In the *pagan* world, a *Ziggurat* was an ancient temple-tower crowned by a throne-summit, typically having a horn (like the altars of YHWH) at each of its four corners. These temple-towers were stylized mountains – replicas of the domains of the gods of their lands, as it was believed that the gods dwelt in mountainous elevations. I have often considered that this perception may have been a residual memory in man of our *first home*, the mountain-garden habitation of *Eden*. Although it is beyond the scope of this book, many scholars believe that Eden must have been an elevated place in order for its four rivers to *flow out* to water the earth (Genesis 2:10-14). Ancient man's construction of these sanctuaries may have been born out of a sin-distorted memory of our first days in God's Edenic mountain-garden habitation where we walked with him before the fall.

ARTIST'S DEPICTION OF THE ZIGGURAT OF UR

From www.bible-history.com/

Figure 3.1

Meredith Kline has described how the temple-tower summit was an area ornamented by horns, symbolizing the domain of the pagan god in power (Kline 2001:60-61).The *Tower of Babel* in Genesis 11 was such a tower and was believed to have been dedicated to the ancient god *Marduk*. The great tower was part of the *Esagila* complex in the ancient city of Babylon. The structure's Sumerian name, *Etemenanki* (E-temen-an-ki), means *house of the foundation of heaven on earth*. The ruins of towers like it still exist in several parts of the world.

The presence of these structures in Zechariah's world is especially significant with respect to Zechariah 1:21, where it states that, as a result of Israel's exile, "no man lifts his head," quite possibly referring to the *destruction of Israel's temple complex*. As a consequence of that event, they believed that their God had been defeated, leaving them no *divine habitation or God to "look up" upon*. The reference to *lifting the head* has an interesting connection to the Esagila temple complex previously mentioned. Again, Meredith Kline has observed that the translation of the Sumerian name *Esagila* is *the house of the lifting up of the head* (Kline 2001:61). The vision speaks in the language of dominion and war among deities. The assumption of the pagan powers in our text was that their *universally powerful gods humiliated and scattered Israel, defeated their God in war, and threw down the temple tower dedicated to his name*. In a word, not only was Israel cast down and scattered, but in the understanding of the ancients, Marduk of the Babylonians had conquered YHWH.

THE FOUR CRAFTSMEN

God's response to the folly of his enemies was to demonstrate that he would dispatch a company which would strike fear in their hearts and defeat them. Strangely, however, those who were sent were not presented to Zechariah as warriors, but *craftsmen*! The Hebrew word translated *craftsmen* is *khawrawsh* (typically a *builder, engraver,* or *worker*). The Greek translation of the Old Testament, called the

Septuagint (abbreviated LXX), translates the Hebrew, *khawrawsh*, as *tekton* in Greek. This is the same Greek word found in the New Testament to describe Jesus as a *carpenter*. What could God have been *redefining* in the understanding of His people as to what strikes fear in the hearts of his enemies, and affects their overthrow as well?

It should be observed that God did not show Zechariah a *solitary warrior-hero*. What he saw was a *company* of four, and they were *builders*. Considering our earlier discussion of the biblical use of the number four, it suggests that builders are a *universal company* - an inclusive company, possibly like the one described as consisting of "every tribe and tongue and people and nation" in Revelation 5:9. Apparently, God wanted Israel to understand that nothing strikes fear in the hearts of his enemies more than an inclusive company *skilled at building!* At this season of Israel's history, like every other time in redemptive history, there was only *one building* on the divine agenda – God's house. It was time to abandon fears, personal aspirations, and differences in order to begin focusing on building the house of God. As soon as that was accomplished and his glory-presence was reestablished in the midst of his people, he would arise on their behalf to defeat His enemies.

CONTEMPORARY RELEVANCE

1. As the New Testament community of faith we must understand first and foremost, that we are called to *build up* the house of God. Zechariah's second vision redefines all conceptions of warfare by teaching that the enemies of God are not defeated by "super saints" or a select group of warriors, but by those who, from the least to the greatest, are fully devoted to one another and engaged in the *work of building*. They bear the image of the *carpenter* from Nazareth who said:

> . . . upon this rock *I will build* My church; and the gates of Hades will not overpower it (Matthew 16:18).

Matthew makes a clear connection between the work of building and warfare. That work is comprised of articulating and building God's Church which reflects his kingdom, the *counter-reality* existing among his people before the very presence of the powers. This requires tremendous faith and vision. Israel was reminded of their vulnerability by temple towers of the gods who seemed to be greater than their own, especially in view of the fact that YHWH's house lay in ruins, while those of their enemies stood forebodingly tall and majestic. We, also, are surrounded by modern day ziggurats, those great skyscrapers, signs, and buildings that testify to the strength of the gods of our age - greed, lust, power, persuasion, and control. In contrast, many of our churches struggle week to week just to financially sustain a modest meeting facility and pastoral oversight. Against the background of such overwhelming displays of human achievement, we may even be tempted to ask, "Where is God?" or "What do we have that can compete against such formidable competition?" Yet, in the face of such enormous obstacles, we are called to engage ourselves in the communal process of *formation* - the building up of the people of God to be a suitable habitation for the one we call the King of Kings and Lord of Lords. We need not compete with the building projects, power, or monetary success of the world around us. The testimony of Christ is not, nor ever has been, in the brick and mortar construction, or any outward appearance of success, no matter how impressive it may appear. The house built for His name now and always will be the gathered Church unified under the banner of Jesus Christ. We are called to build people together, nurtured, focused, and unified. Against such a company of carpenters, no enemy of God can stand.

It is clear therefore, that such a confrontation requires more than our Sunday-go-to-meeting Christian experience. Building is messy, most often inconvenient, frequently accomplished outside of the church building, and hardly ever among the people with which we might personally *choose* to build. God rarely demonstrates a willingness to accommodate our busy personal schedule, but as in the parable of the *Good Samaritan*, he purposely brings people, situations, and opportunities before us at the most inopportune times. That requires, especially for those of us in the West, a new flexibility and focus, to remind ourselves that we have been called of God not to serve ourselves but to "build" others. This can be taxing, and potentially demanding of all that we have. Jesus used the very combination of metaphors of which we speak - building and warfare - in a succinct, almost startling declaration concerning the all-consuming demands of discipleship:

> For which of you, desiring to build a tower, does not first sit down and count the cost, whether he has enough to complete it? Otherwise, when he has laid a foundation and is not able to finish, all who see it begin to mock him, saying, "This man began to build and was not able to finish." Or what king, going out to encounter another king in war, will not sit down first and deliberate whether he is able with ten thousand to meet him who comes against him with twenty thousand? And if not, while the other is yet a great way off, he sends a delegation and asks for terms of peace. So therefore, any one of you who does not renounce all that he has cannot be my disciple (Luke 14:28-33 ESV).

The Lord Jesus did not speak these things because he wants us to live in abject poverty. He was warning us against being chained to the obligations of this life to such an extent that we simply cannot meet the rigorous demands of *building* and *warfare*. They are not weekend endeavors, but a way of life for those whose hearts have been smitten with a passion for the vision of God, and share his love for the hopeless and the lost.

2. The great restoration promise of Isaiah 2:4, stated: "and never again will they learn war." It is worth pausing to consider the possibility that Isaiah wasn't looking at a millennial (one thousand year) period of *world peace*, but a time in redemptive history when there would be peace among the inhabitants of the *global mountain of God* (v. 2-3).

Isaiah's visionary mountain was a prefiguration of the *dominion of the Lord Jesus Christ*, which has now emerged throughout the world as also foreseen by the prophet Daniel:

> …But the stone that struck the statue became *a great mountain* and filled the whole earth (Daniel 2:35).

The people of God, as communities of faith throughout the world, have sprung up in every nation to be trained, not only to *war*, but to *build*. Consider the words of Paul to the Ephesians:

> And He gave some as apostles, and some as prophets, and some as evangelists, and some as pastors and teachers, for the equipping of the saints for the work of service, to the *building up of the body of Christ*, until we all attain to the unity of the faith, and of the knowledge of the Son of God, to a mature man, to the measure of the stature which belongs to the fullness of Christ. As a result, we are no longer to be children, tossed here and there by waves and carried about by every wind of doctrine, by the trickery of men, by craftiness in deceitful scheming; but speaking the truth in love, we are to grow up in all aspects into Him who is the head, even Christ, from whom the whole body, being fitted and held together by what every joint supplies, according to the proper working of each individual part, causes the growth of the body for the *building up of itself* in love (Ephesians 4:11-16).

Contrary to what some might believe, the church's first order of business is not to make Christianity *as convenient as possible* for its members. The apostle rolls out God's grand design of five-fold leadership to prepare the saints *to do the work* of the ministry, which is to *build itself (his body)* into the image of Christ. This happens when *everyone* contributes by employing God-given callings, gifts, talents, and resources. It calls us to participate in something greater than ourselves that demands the fullness of our love, loyalty, and energy. This is not merely *private religious piety*, but the pouring out of ourselves in love on behalf of others. But who has the time? Like the soul on whom the seed fell, but whose growth and fruitfulness was inhibited by the thorny growth (Mark 4:18-19), our lives are consumed with earning, buying, selling, and a host of domestic pursuits that utterly choke our capacity to give of ourselves to the degree necessary to truly accomplish the divine objective. It is no small task, particularly in a society where individualism, personal peace, and prosperity are the idolatrous sacred cows of our age, and the privatized pursuit of personal well-being is the foundational creed that nurtures western culture. Most tragic of all is the *mistaken assumption* on the part of many of God's people that these cultural values - or for that matter, *any* culture's values - are consistent with Christian values. After all, we are the good guys. Of course God is on our side! Unfortunately, the only god who is on the side of a greed-dependent culture rooted in production and consumption, is called by the ancient name of *Mammon* (Matthew 6:24).

Carpenters Before the Powers

Paul emphasizes building, faith, knowledge, the divine image, truth, and most importantly, love. The communities are to be characterized by other-affirming love. The local church is to be the place where human community is perfected in love. God's desire is to put this exemplary community, perfected in love, on display as a demonstration of his original intention for man. Earlier in this letter to the Ephesians, Paul asserts that this is the mystery and the eternal purpose of God - that this diverse community would display His multifaceted wisdom before all principalities and powers.

> To me, the very least of all saints, this grace was given, to preach to the Gentiles the unfathomable riches of Christ, and to bring to light what is the administration of the mystery which for ages has been hidden in God who created all things; so that the manifold wisdom

of God might now be made known through the church to the rulers and the authorities in the heavenly places. This was in accordance with the eternal purpose which He carried out in Christ Jesus our Lord, (Ephesians 3:8-11).

That is to say that God will accomplish what no political ideology or governmental system has ever accomplished through political strategy, money, and power. He will perfect and unify a diverse remnant of the human community in Christ through the agency of his own Spirit and wisdom, and display it before the entities that rule every manner of power center in the world. Although we don't understand exactly when or in what precise manner this reality will fully materialize, we must embrace *that it is God's grand design*. Various eschatological schemes have been entertained throughout the Church's history, none of which have gained universal acceptance. However, one thing appears certain, whether it be in this age or the one to come; Paul is not teaching the Ephesians that God is presenting his handiwork to *indistinct angelic entities hovering about in the atmosphere*, but that that those other-worldly powers and principalities are integrated into this world's political, socio-economic, and cultural systems. Charles L. Campbell writes concerning the role of the powers:

> While not denying . . . spiritual realities . . . I focus on the activity of powers as they are spiritually *at work in and through concrete material institutions and systems in the world.* This is how the powers shape the lives of most of the people to whom I preach. I thus emphasize the central spiritual dimension of the powers, but not as spiritual beings existing and working independently of material structures in the world (Campbell 2002:15).

As does Walter Wink:

The "principalities and powers" are the inner and outer aspects of any given manifestations of power. As the inner aspect they are the spirituality of institutions, the "within" of corporate structures and systems, the inner essence of outer organizations of power. As the outer aspect they are political systems, appointed officials, the "chair" of an organization, laws - in short, all the tangible manifestations which power takes. Power tends to have a visible pole, and outer form - be it a church, a nation, or an economy -and an invisible pole, and inner spirit or driving force that animates, legitimates, and regulates its physical manifestation in the world (Wink 1984:8).

As a model social entity in every nation of the world, the Church is on display with a mission to demonstrate (within itself) how human society was intended to function, not as a result of the implementation of human political ideologies, manipulation, and power mongering which serve the interests of *man*, but as reflection or the love and wisdom of the living God. This holy community exists as a result of an inner transformation of the hearts of its citizens by the Holy Spirit who has been given to us as a result of the life and ministry of the Lord Jesus.

3. The principalities and powers, or *horns*, hinder the people of God by attempting to keep us chained to cultural, national, and socioeconomic values and norms by which many of us mistakenly continue to derive our identity. We allow ourselves be defined by culture, nationality, skin color, occupation, gender, and even the favorable or unfavorable opinions family or peers; never thinking for a moment that we are still chained to our *old man* who was crucified with Christ. With that in view, it is of no small theological significance that Israel's exile meant being overtaken by *the Babylonians* (Chaldeans). Babylon was the *origin of the idolatrous cultural heritage of their father-patriarch, Abraham, out of which he was called.*

Terah took Abram his son, and Lot the son of Haran, his grandson, and Sarai his daughter-in-law, his son Abram's wife; and *they went out together from Ur of the Chaldeans* in order to enter the land of Canaan; and they went as far as Haran, and settled there (Genesis 11:31).

Joshua said to all the people, "Thus says the LORD, the God of Israel, From ancient times your fathers lived beyond the River, namely,
Terah, the father of Abraham and the father of Nahor, and *they
served other gods*" (Joshua 24:2).

Just as Israel's slavery in Egypt characterizes our bondage to sin,
the Babylonian Captivity characterizes our imprisonment to racial,
cultural, national identities and loyalties; from which the scriptures ex-
hort us to *free ourselves:*

Awake, awake,
Clothe yourself in your strength, O Zion;
Clothe yourself in your beautiful garments,
O Jerusalem, the holy city;
For the uncircumcised and the unclean will no longer come
into you.
Shake yourself from the dust, rise up,
O captive Jerusalem;
Loose yourself from the chains [*of Babylon*] around your neck,
O captive daughter of Zion (Isaiah 52:1-2; cf. Zechariah 2:6-7).

The powers are "gods" in their own right, having agendas, ideologies, strategies, and visions of control, but none has ever permanently
accomplished authentic, lasting, well-being and harmony on the earth.
Neither *can* they accomplish such lofty ideals because those ideals are
merely a *facade* behind which greed and lust for power and control
lurk. When Israel demanded of Samuel to give them a king and *to
be like other nations*, they foolishly assumed that this would involve a
mere change in political structure and more security. However, once
the transition began, it *brought with it all the systems employed by the powers
to shape men under their control.* That is to suggest that the forces expelled
in their deliverance from Egypt, once readmitted on a national scale,
brought along "seven – even more evil – making the latter state worse
than the first" What is often overlooked in the following commonly

quoted text is that it is an indictment of the entire nation of Israel in the day of Jesus, not merely an individual or personal lesson:

> "Now when the unclean spirit goes out of a man, it passes through waterless places seeking rest, and does not find it. " Then it says, 'I will return to my house from which I came'; and when it comes, it finds it unoccupied, swept, and put in order. "Then it goes and takes along with it seven other spirits more wicked than itself, and they go in and live there; and the last state of that man becomes worse than the first. *That is the way it will also be with this evil generation*" (Matthew 12:43-45).

In contrast, God ordained that his original intention for his creation would be realized and on display through personal, social, economic, and spiritual relationships within the Church. This is what we are called to build. We must not assume that the people of God will passively observe these things happen by themselves. We are called to exercise *intentionality* in building bridges to one another - absorbing the distance that exists because of those differences. This must involve infinitely more than Sunday morning backslapping. We must seek out and rectify both ethnical and economic imbalances and employ (build) ministry processes that ensure that those who have been marginalized for any reason are being nurtured *holistically* (with respect to the whole person) in the body of Christ.

4. God has placed leadership in the Church, a five-fold ministry to be precise, to prepare us for the work of the ministry concerning which he says, "every joint supplies" (Ephesians 4:16). Every part contributes. Paul introduces the fresh New Testament paradigm of the *living body* - the Church - which is the true temple of the living God. The forces at work against that effort are relentlessly competing for possession of our hearts, minds, and the work of our hands. In the face of this, we have been commissioned to build thriving Christian communities where an alternative social reality is on display. The Church is to embody now,

in seed form, the very presence of the future. The great commission enjoins us not to simply *save souls* but to *make disciples* in all the nations:

> And Jesus came up and spoke to them, saying, "All authority has been given to Me in heaven and on earth. Go therefore and make disciples of all the nations, baptizing them in the name of the Father and the Son and the Holy Spirit, teaching them to observe all that I commanded you; and lo, I am with you always, even to the end of the age" (Matthew 28:18-20).

The foundation for that discipleship is to teach all that Jesus Himself commanded. This is called *formation*:

> This process of shaping the habits, affections, and dispositions of people – when it is done by the Christian tradition – is called formation. It is a communal process similar to a craft apprenticeship, in which newcomers learn the explicit and tacit knowledge of practitioners by a process of imitation, then internalization, then innovation. Over time, if formation is successful newcomers themselves become adept in encountering, imagining, and reasoning through Christian eyes, minds, and hearts...Stressing the centrality of formation in Christianity underscores two important points: that Christianity depends on collective, intensive practices distinct from the non-Christian world for its perpetuation; and that the process of "making Christians" is always a precarious matter, which can be undermined or diluted by other powerful institutions and processes of "formation."... Where formation has been neglected, undermined, or done poorly, evidence of such inadequacies appears as pathologies in the body of Christ and its practices, priorities, and affections... Our primary assertion is this: to the extent that capitalist formation succeeds, Christian formation fails (Budde 2002:60-61).

The authors, who are clearly focusing on Western culture, identify *capitalist* formation in opposition to *biblical* formation; however the truth they present must be understood as a challenge to the Church operating in *any* political, economic, or corporate system. Socialism, communism, fascism, conservatism, liberalism and virtually every other ideology known to man is in direct competition with God's kingdom purposes, resulting in the need for building biblically based formational processes in the community of faith regardless of the nation into which we are planted. As Stanley Hauerwas has observed:

> The church does not exist to provide an ethos [moral character] for democracy or any other form of social organization, but stands as a political alternative to every nation, witnessing to the kind of social life possible for *those that have been formed by the story of Christ* (Hauerwas 2001).

Given these enormous implications, it is not difficult to understand why God's *builders* strike fear in the hearts of the powers. As we work toward building the body into the image of Christ, we are also wrenching God's people from the influence of every other wind of "doctrine" and the grips of powerful strongholds of idolatry, greed, arrogance, and sensuality that characterize the fallen world. When we immerse our lives in formational processes that align hearts and minds of disciples with the alternative kingdom-community vision of God, we draw nearer to the fulfillment of his ultimate purpose - the exaltation and display of his holy nation of priests above all the kingdoms of this present age. This grand and lofty vision can and will be realized, but it must begin first in our own local Christian communities, one neighborhood at a time.

Chapter 4

THE THIRD VISION
I SPREAD YOU OUT

Zechariah's visionary perspective suddenly moved away from the environment of the nations to the vicinity of Jerusalem. There he observed a *young man* (undoubtedly an angel) with a measuring instrument about to measure the site of the city. Another angel came on the scene with urgent instructions to put a halt to the measuring, which initiated a startling prophetic oracle conveying YHWH's plan to do something entirely new and unexpected.

> Then I lifted up my eyes and looked, and behold, there was a man with a measuring line in his hand. So I said, "Where are you going?" And he said to me, "To measure Jerusalem, to see how wide it is and how long it is." And behold, the angel who was speaking with me was going out, and another angel was coming out to meet him, and said to him, "Run, speak to that young man, saying, 'Jerusalem will be inhabited without walls because of the multitude of men and cattle within it. For I,' declares the LORD, 'will be a wall of fire around her, and I will be the glory in her midst'" (Zechariah 2:1-5).

MEASURING THE CITY

Zechariah was given the opportunity to interact with the angel who was about to measure the city. Most commentators agree that the actual, physical structure had not yet been built at the time of this vision, therefore, it is a reasonable conclusion that the city was not *physical* but instead an *ideal* Jerusalem. It is also plausible that the angel was merely measuring the *site* for rebuilding purposes. J. B. Rotherham's

Emphasized Bible (Rotherham 1994) captures the *spirit* of the text in his translation of verse two:

> ...to measure Jerusalem, to see what [should be] the breadth there-of and what the length thereof (Zechariah 2:2b-*brackets are part of the translation*).

Similarly, the Jewish Publication Society (JPS) *Tanakh* (Berlin 1999) translates the same verse as follows:

> "...to measure Jerusalem," he replied, "to see how long and wide *it is to be*" (Zechariah 2:6 in the Hebrew Bible).

Zechariah was witnessing a concerted effort to ensure that Jerusalem's ancient boundaries were properly reestablished. Now that God was moving again, it was imperative that the city be rebuilt precisely to the specifications of its former days - its size, shape, dimensions, and features had to be exactly the same. However, in the middle of the commotion, a *third* angel was sent to put a stop to the evaluation. He moved with a sense of urgency that is evidenced by the double imperative – *Run! Speak...!* (Merrill: bible.org). Not only was this an urgent command, but so urgent that it was given to Zechariah's *host* angel, entreating *him* to step into the vision and put an immediate halt to the measuring process.

Knowing that these angelic beings are messengers of YHWH who are dispatched to do his bidding (Hebrews 1:14), it would be natural to ask why he would dispatch them with such blatantly contradicting missions, to which Eugene Merrill answers:

> ...the point of the prophetic vision is not to instruct an inexperienced angel, but the prophet himself. It is Zechariah who must understand that the city to come will spill out over its ancient walls and that YHWH will become the wall... (Merrill: bible.org).

It appears that God desired for his prophet to observe three very important things that materialize in a crisis of reorientation. *First*, there is a natural human tendency to look back at what "Jerusalem" was and wrongly assume that God intends for the future to look like the past. *Second*, it is the grace of God to intervene, not only for *our* sake, but to ensure that we are embracing *his* vision in order to fulfill *his* purposes. Our nostalgic longing to recover the past merely serves to paralyze us and keep us from what God is doing now. *Third*, once he has foiled the *human* undertaking, he articulates new possibilities to enlarge our thinking, offering a creative new vision for our future.

The angel with the measuring rod was sent by YHWH to demonstrate our tendency to look at the past through rose-colored glasses as if it were an *ideal*. Our selective memory tends to reflect on the good things - *how great it used to be* - because our heart's desire is to reaffirm its value. We do such things, of course, to justify the hopeful reconstruction of the old, comfortable, and familiar places that are now lost, not realizing that it was *God himself who caused*, or - if you prefer - *allowed*, the loss to occur. Like Israel, we *remember* the goodness of God's dealings with us but forget that our responses to his grace were often apathetic, inconsistent, and selfish, albeit often due to ignorance. God does not hold our old mistakes over our heads, yet he must change our life and response patterns if we are going to become aligned with the desires of *his* heart. What YHWH was about to do would not resemble Israel's old model contained in walls of exclusivity and privilege. The ideal city about to be described was a city that could not be contained in those ancient, rigid barriers by which the nation defined herself. It would be a city *without the walls that exclude others*, having capacity to embrace the multitudes of people from various cultures and an abundance of blessing that could not be contained in the older wineskin.

My own life stands as humble illustration of the point. As of this writing, eight years have elapsed since my own crisis began. During those years, I have come to know, love, and enter into authentic relationships with people of diverse socio-economic and racial backgrounds in

ways previously unheard of. My own redefinition as a man has resulted
in true enlargement, first of my heart's capacity to embrace *the other*,
followed by doors of opportunity to expand personal influence among
Christians and non-Christians of entirely foreign socio-economic environments, *especially* urban minorities. It is deeply humbling to look
back and see the fingerprint of God in all of the circumstances he used
to alter the wellspring of a human heart.

The city of Jerusalem would eventually be rebuilt along with the
temple, but God was seeking to communicate to his people that his
universal vision, the *ideal* Jerusalem, was much larger, much grander,
and much more inclusive than that. Joyce Baldwin captures the true
sense of verse three:

> ...Jerusalem will be as *open villages* without walls, open to all who
> wish to enter (Eze. 38:11), free from dividing walls and national bar-
> riers, knowing no limits on the size of its population. Far from being
> exclusive, Zechariah opens the city of God to a multitude of men
> and cattle (Baldwin 1972:106).

The description as *open villages without walls* is consistent with both
the *King James Bible* and *Young's Literal Translation*. *Green's Literal Version*
similarly translates the Hebrew as "unwalled villages." This offers an
insightful image of the redefined character of the people of God. We
see a new definition of the city of God emerging from this vision, as
well as an enlargement of the nation as it begins to present itself and
its God in all the nations of the earth. However, in the ancient world,
unwalled villages were not the safest place to raise a family. Without
the protection of city walls, a village was vulnerable to any type of
predator, be it man or beast. The potential vulnerability that accompanied such a loosely defined, universal reality would raise questions
in the mind of the prophet as well as his audience, so the Lord affirms
that the city would not be protected by *stone* walls, but that *he, himself*
would be to Jerusalem a *surrounding wall of fire*. In the Hebrew text of

Zechariah 2:5, ("I . . . will be . . ."), the word *I* is *emphatic* (Baldwin 1972:106). This divine reassurance is not only significant because Israel was weaker and possibly more vulnerable than at any time other in her national history, but it is also the emphatic declaration of the living God that *his purposes will stand*. He has never been defeated, nor can he be. His counsels are not dependent upon the relative strength or weakness of man. The consuming fire of his eternal power will surround the frail remnant of his people to the end that they will yet accomplish that to which they were destined.

FLEE BABYLON

"Ho there! Flee from the land of the north," declares the LORD, "for I have dispersed you as the four winds of the heavens," declares the LORD. "Ho, Zion! Escape, you who are living with the daughter of Babylon." For thus says the LORD of hosts, "After glory He has sent me against the nations which plunder you, for he who touches you, touches the apple of His eye. For behold, I will wave My hand over them so that they will be plunder for their slaves. Then you will know that the LORD of hosts has sent Me. Sing for joy and be glad, O daughter of Zion; for behold I am coming and I will dwell in your midst," declares the LORD. "Many nations will join themselves to the LORD in that day and will become My people. Then I will dwell in your midst, and you will know that the LORD of hosts has sent Me to you. The LORD will possess Judah as His portion in the holy land, and will again choose Jerusalem. Be silent, all flesh, before the LORD; for He is aroused from His holy habitation" (Zechariah 2:6-13).

The historical context of verses 6 through 13 is the imminent judgment of God that was coming upon the city of Babylon at the hand of Darius, king of Persia. Darius was about to destroy the city which had been captured but not destroyed by King Cyrus when he defeated the Chaldean Empire 20 years earlier. Verses six and seven constitute a warning cry to those who were *living* (Hebrew: *yashab* – sitting, remaining, or dwelling) in Babylon - that is to those who were comfortable, had become accustomed to exile, and who chose to remain there. Their place in Babylon allowed them to go to synagogue to study Torah and retain an element of distinction as a people, safe, sound, and risk-free. Many had found places in the business community and built stable lives for their families. Yet YHWH's house remained in a state of desolation. Babylon was never intended to be a *permanent* place of residence for the people of God, but it had become *just that* to the vast majority of Israelites who remained there in contrast to the relatively small number who had returned to the holy land. The following is from the *Anchor Bible Commentary*:

> Any number of reasons might explain why many Judahites would not be eager to return home to Palestine. First and perhaps foremost, some of them had achieved a good measure of success in Babylon and could not face the uncertainty of returning to an area devastated by earlier wars. In addition, the . . . forms of . . . tradition which they would encounter upon their return would not necessarily be compatible with an openness to the adjusted Babylonian forms (Meyers 1987: xxxvii).

Why would anyone want to throw away a religious culture that had evolved into such safe, predictable, and stable state of affairs? What would be gained by risking everything for a three month trek to the *ruins* of Jerusalem and the old religion of their grandparents? The call, however, was an alarm to awaken from their sleep and their comforts and to flee the city. The *urgency* of the appeal was a warning not to remain comfortable there but to escape the city that was about to be judged and destroyed. The injunction of the Lord continued with a statement that it was not merely *their* comfort and convenience that was at stake, but *his own* glory. His name had been slandered and his house and city plundered by this arrogant Chaldean nation. The time had come for them to cease benefitting from Babylon's wealth and power. YHWH was about to arise and execute his vengeance on them in order for Israel to know that Babylon's victory was no victory at all (the perception addressed in the second vision), but instead *an assignment by the living God* who had given them only temporary jurisdiction over his people. Parenthetically, this is also a remarkable prefiguration of the *cross*, where the *apparent defeat* of Jesus by the enemies of God became the venue or means by which those very enemies – the principalities and powers of sin and death - were defeated.

The rebuilding of YHWH's house which was about to occur simultaneously with the destruction of Babylon was to be an occasion of great joy for the Jews. It meant that the glory that had departed from them in the days of Ezekiel (cf. Ezekiel 10:18) was about to return to the temple that bore his name. Additionally, the statement in verse 11 that, "many nations will join themselves to the LORD in that day and become my people" is pregnant with meaning, being a definitive declaration of YHWH's intent to enlarge them into an all-inclusive people.

To understand this, it is necessary to observe an interesting peculiarity in the Hebrew text between Zechariah 2:6 (this context) and an earlier statement in Zechariah 1:19-21 (the context of the *horns* and the *craftsmen*). In the vision of the four horns, the prophet employed the Hebrew word *zawrah* (1:19, 21), which means to *toss, winnow, or scatter like chaff from grain*, to indicate that the horns had *scattered* the people of God. However, in this vision he used the Hebrew word *pawras* (2:6), which means to *spread out*. The distinction indicates that the nations foolishly assumed that they had hopelessly scattered the nation of God, forever diffusing their power. The truth of the matter is they had been unwittingly used of God to judge his nation. As a result of that purification and exile, Jewish presence and influence would be *spread out* or *enlarged* as they planted God-fearing communities into every nation they went. The "powers" may have scattered the people, but in reality God was merely spreading them out. This is how God began his mission of obtaining glory for himself among the nations. The uniqueness and the particularity of Israel even from its beginning had a *universalistic* purpose; that through them (the seed of Abraham) *all* the nations of the earth might be blessed. This, of course, would be fully realized through the true seed of Abraham, the Lord Jesus Christ. Israel had neither the heart to understand nor the eyes to see (Isaiah 6:9), but here in Zechariah 2:9, God assured them that once the outcome was realized in the context of history, they would begin to understand. So it was that many Jews became believers in Christ as a result of his public ministry and those of the apostles after him. There is ample evidence of this in the gospels as well as the Book of Acts.

CONTEMPORARY RELEVANCE

For the earth will be filled with the knowledge of the glory of the LORD, as the waters cover the sea (Habakkuk 2:14).

1. God is on a mission. Passages like Habakkuk 2:14 tell us of God's desire to spread his people out to influence the world with the gospel. However, we read passages like this thinking that somehow this condition will simply emerge in human history apart from God's agent of the mission - the Church. Worse yet, that it will be realized after we have begun to sprout wings in the *great by-and-by*. These are inadequate options. The vision of God as spoken through the prophet comes about not only through intentional activity by the Church to fulfill her mission, but also by God's forcing hand to drive us toward the mission. When we become comfortable or dull of hearing, he must stretch us and move us from our places of comfort, security, and self-centeredness into places we would not otherwise choose to go. Although he loves his people and is certainly concerned with their well-being, this is not his overriding objective. *It is the expansion of his glory and his name to all the nations of the earth that drives those dealings with his people who have been called to participate in the mission.* Unfortunately, he must often allow the safe and secure walls to be torn down in order for enlargement to occur.

2. *The measuring angel* had to be stopped cold when he attempted to assess and measure what needed to be done to restore *old* Jerusalem. Thus, it stands that we can still miss God's message by attempting to cling to or rebuild old paradigms. How often we seek, especially in the aftermath of crisis, to rebuild our sense of security by looking back to the things that are comfortable; seeking to recover those personal, financial, and emotional losses – because that recovery affects *things that can be seen and touched* - those things that make us feel secure.

In the midst of the crisis of losing my home, my family was helping with the packing of all my belongings, deciding what should be kept and what had to be given away or sold. I recall the moment when, embarrassingly, in front of the entire family, I dropped onto the floor like a spoiled child and began to cry, "I want my life back!" I was happy to be with Jesus, but broken by the cost incurred because of that relationship. Bear in mind that the move had to be made within 24 hours, and there was as yet no place for me to live. Of course, no one in my family would have allowed me to end up on the street, but as a man of 50 who had known international travel, a little prestige, and a relatively successful career, I could not at the time see any comfort in that. I wanted Jesus, but I wanted to feel the old familiar turf under my feet to which I had become accustomed. God would not have it, although, he (not surprisingly) came through in the 11th hour with a rental home but not without demonstrating to me how willing he is to utterly undo our carnal sense of security and force us out into a position of vulnerability. In that place we have no alternative but to trust in him who is unseen, knowing that he is not limited by our absence of resources.

Corporately, Christendom as we know it is slowly moving into the sunset as a new *postmodern* era has arisen. Churches in North America are losing their status of unquestioned social respectability and being challenged for the first time since the middle ages by an emerging *pluralism*. The White-Anglo-Saxon-Protestant dominant religious culture of this part of the world has been weighed in the balance and found wanting. Stanley Grenz observes that this cultural shift is not unlike the birth of *modernity* which arose out of the Reformation:

> Many social observers agree that the Western world is in the midst of change. In fact, we are experiencing a cultural shift that rivals the innovations that marked the birth of modernity out of the decay of the Middle Ages: we are in the midst of transition from the modern to the postmodern era (Grenz 1996:2).

It is a time for us to either remain entrenched in modernity, or open our hearts to new possibilities for interaction with the emerging post-modern culture around us. If we remain locked in the old norms, we will eventually consign ourselves to irrelevancy. Many churches today are already bemoaning the loss of the next generation who believe in Jesus, but find their church community unable to offer anything relevant. This is neither justification nor condemnation of either side, merely an *observation* of what is taking place. Willingness to reexamine how we do church does not mean that we compromise the truth of the gospel of Jesus Christ. It means that we open our hearts to a less structured, more relational and multicultural community life and witness. We must adapt to and invest ourselves in our surrounding neighborhoods rather than thinking, "If we build it, they will come." What we do on Sunday mornings means nothing to our neighbors if we are merely driving in from 10 or 20 miles away, having "church," and going home to our safe, secure, and undisrupted lives. A relevant church is one that is willing to get involved with the messiness of the broken lives God wants to heal – particularly in the neighborhoods to which he has called us to labor and worship.

3. Like the ancient nation of Israel facing a *crisis of reorientation*, God's people must always realize that we are *the apple (pupil) of God's eye*. The actions of *judgment, crisis, and reorientation* are those of a loving father disciplining his children (Hebrews 12:9-10) in order that they might walk in holiness and singleness of purpose. He always has in

mind the spread of the gospel. The dispersion of the nation of Israel through exile ultimately meant that synagogues were built and Jewish communities established throughout the civilized world. This was of staggering significance for the spread of the gospel by the early church several hundred years later. After the death and resurrection of the Lord Jesus, the apostles were endowed with the promise of the Holy Spirit to enable them to preach and spread the gospel with power in every nation. In each place where they were called, many non-Jews (biblically referred to as God-fearers) became familiar with the God of Israel and the promise of a Messiah because of the Jewish communities which had started being established four to five centuries earlier. This is evident in the Book of Acts:

> But going on from Perga, they arrived at Pisidian Antioch, and on the Sabbath day they *went into the synagogue* and sat down... Now when the meeting of the synagogue had broken up, many of the Jews and of the *God-fearing proselytes* [converts]followed Paul and Barnabas, who, speaking to them, were urging them to continue in the grace of God (Acts 13:14, 43).

> Now when they had traveled through Amphipolis and Apollonia, they came to Thessalonica, where there was *a synagogue of the Jews*... And some of them were persuaded and joined Paul and Silas, along with *a large number of the God-fearing Greeks* and a number of the leading women (Acts 17:1, 4).

4. How often it is that we seek God for revival and renewal in our families, churches, and communities. However, when God's wind begins to blow - shaking up our comfortable and established norms to make room for a new wave of divine revelation and power - we desperately cling to that which we have known, resisting the process of being poured out into new wineskins. Recent history bears witness to the fact that during the *Jesus movement* of the 1970s, it was observed that many established, full gospel churches resisted the move of God

because those of us coming into the Church had long hair and wore blue jeans. The *Charismatic Movement* that came on its heels was too *Catholic*. The *renewal* of the 1990s was resisted as too fanatical. The recent emphasis of the Spirit on relationships, community development, and social justice is resisted by some as a *social* gospel. Throughout the history of the Church, the pattern has been evident. We stubbornly insist that what is to come must look like what has been in the past.

Every movement of the Holy Spirit will have its fringe extremists, and the character of the whole must not be measured by either its conformance to past norms or the behavior of extremists. God is always in the business of *redefining and enlarging*; creating new possibilities and making his truth relevant in new social contexts. Yesterday's *wheat* is today's *husk*, which in time must be removed as new wheat springs forth. Those who cling to old norms, in spite of the fact that their community has become a stale, dwindling relic of the past, will find themselves stoically smug in their "correctness," missing out on the joy and dynamics of a new direction of God.

THE JOURNEY CONTINUES . . .

Thus far our prophet has seen visions from the vantage point of the surrounding nations and the land. His people responded in repentance to the word he had spoken to them, opening the visionary door for the prophet to see what YHWH was preparing for them. The great cedar had fallen to the Babylonian armies. After two generations, a lowly myrtle sprang up but in a dubious and uncertain place. Although they were weak and vulnerable, Zechariah was encouraged. Among the mounted messengers of YHWH who had been traversing throughout the land stood the *White Horse Rider* ready to deliver YHWH's frail remnant. Then, he heard the voice of his God who was giving assurance that he would again raise up his place of habitation on Mount Zion.

Next, he saw God's plan to overthrow the powers who scattered his people. This overthrow would be accomplished without so much as a sword raised in Israel. As craftsmen, God's people would focus on *building* God's house, and when that was accomplished, YHWH would decree from his reestablished throne the destruction of the city of Babylon, with its temple tower, by the hand of the Persian king, Darius.

In the third vision, Zechariah journeyed to the City of Jerusalem, where he saw and heard the admonition of the Lord not to build according to its previous design. The old walls of exclusivity and privilege would be no more. The new heavenly city was going to spring up as a presence without walls in every nation under heaven and would attract and welcome the gentiles in all the nations. Furthermore, the apparent vulnerability of this post-exilic community of faith would be of no concern because YHWH *himself* would be a wall of fire around his people.

Zechariah's journey was about to take him to the central sanctuary – the very throne room of YHWH, of which the earthly temple was a mere copy. It was there that Zechariah would observe before his own eyes, the central conflict of history. Man, his advocate, and his accuser are standing before the judgment seat of YHWH.

Chapter 5

THE FOURTH & FIFTH VISIONS THE SANCTUARY ENCOUNTER

Heaven and earth suddenly merged as the prophet was afforded a view of the very courtroom of YHWH himself. In this scene, Joshua, the current high priest of Israel, stood before the Lord in the central sanctuary, with the defending angel at his right hand. Satan, the accuser whose name is derived from the Hebrew term *ha-satan*, meaning *the adversary*, was also present on his opposite side with an agenda of his own.

> Then he showed me Joshua the high priest standing before the angel of the LORD, and Satan standing at his right hand to accuse him. The LORD said to Satan, "The LORD rebuke you, Satan! Indeed, the LORD who has chosen Jerusalem rebuke you! Is this not a brand plucked from the fire?" Now Joshua was clothed with filthy garments and standing before the angel. He spoke and said to those who were standing before him, saying, "Remove the filthy garments from him." Again he said to him, "See, I have taken your iniquity away from you and will clothe you with festal robes" (Zechariah 3:1-4).

THE LORD REBUKE YOU!

The Jews understood the temple complex as a replica of the world, with the central sanctuary at its hub. Josephus, the first century Jewish historian, explains:

> ... for if any one do without prejudice, and with judgment, look upon these things, he will find they were every one made in way of imitation and representation of the universe. When Moses distinguished

the tabernacle into three parts, and allowed two of them to the priests, as a place accessible and common, he denoted the land and the sea, these being of general access to all; but set apart the third division [Holy of Holies] for God, because heaven is inaccessible to men... (Whiston 1987:90 – Translation of Josephus' *Antiquities* 3:7:7).

Centuries before Josephus' time, the prophet Isaiah powerfully articulated the purpose of God for the community of faith, announcing how YHWH had prepared for himself a place of habitation that would be among his people a *planting of heaven* itself:

And I have put My words in your mouth;
I have covered you with the shadow of My hand,
That I may *plant the heavens*,
Lay the foundations of the earth,
And say to Zion, "You are My people" (Isaiah 51:16 NKJV).

Over 60 years had passed since the earthly sanctuary - the replica of heaven - was destroyed. Despite the fact that the Jews were released from their captivity, there had been no shedding of blood to provide cleansing of their sins before YHWH. The sacrificial offerings of the temple ministry had ceased, including the ritual cleansing of the people on the annual *Day of Atonement*. Now, Zechariah was allowed to see the "holiest" man in Israel in his true state before the holiness of God – standing not in the *facsimile* on earth, but in the *true* temple – the heavenly one. As high priest, Joshua stood as a proxy for the state of the whole nation as well. No amount of Bible study or righteous acts could atone for the sins of the people; this required the shedding of blood for, "without the shedding of blood there is no remission" (Hebrews 9:22). Joshua stood hopelessly covered in the filth of the sins of the nation that had accumulated for more than a generation, the extent of which is suggested in the word translated *filthy* in our text. The Hebrew word used is *tso* (or *tsoi*), which comes from the word *tsaw-aw*, meaning *soiled by human excrement*.

There is a subplot in this scene, in which the accuser attempts to bind God in a judicial *catch 22*. As long as the earthly temple remained in ruins, there was no means by which the ceremonial cleansing of the high priest could be accomplished. According to Exodus 29:1-46, the ordination of the high priest's consecration required the use of numerous tabernacle/temple accoutrements such as the laver and the altar of sacrifice which were in the courtyard and the anointing oil, which was a precise mixture specified in Exodus 30:23-25. Below is a selected portion of the entire ceremony:

> (1) Now this is what you shall do to them *to consecrate them to minister as priests to me:* take one young bull and two rams without blemish... (4) Then you shall bring Aaron and his sons to the *doorway of the tent of meeting and wash them with water...* (7) Then you shall take the *anointing oil* and pour it on his head and anoint him... (11) You shall slaughter the bull before the LORD at the doorway of the tent of meeting. (12) You shall take some of the blood of the bull and put it on the horns of the altar with your finger; and you shall pour out all the blood at the base of the altar... (16) And you shall slaughter the ram and shall *take its blood and sprinkle it around on the altar* ... (18) You shall offer up in smoke the whole ram *on the altar; it is a burnt offering to the LORD...* (Excerpts from Exodus 29:1-46).

The adversary would have presented the argument that under the jurisdiction of Moses, YHWH's habitation must be built first, and then the priesthood consecrated using its facilities. In the current dilemma, there was *no existing facility* through which Joshua could be cleansed and consecrated. The reverse was also true. With no sanctified high priest, the services of a newly built temple could not be carried out - the priesthood was *defiled*. The accuser must have argued vehemently that he had *legal ground* with which to bind the hands of God by his own law and place the whole remnant of Israel under a state of condemnation. Of course, being in that state would effectively exempt them from God's blessing and their divinely ordained role in his redemptive plan. This scenario is reflected in the 109th Psalm which condemns the wicked:

> Appoint a wicked man over him,
> And let an accuser stand at his right hand.
> When he is judged, let him come forth guilty,
> And let his prayer become sin.
> Let his days be few;
> Let another take his office (Psalm 109:6-8).

The condemnation of the remnant of Israel would have had staggering consequences. As the holy seed of Abraham who was the carrier of the seed of the woman prophesied in Genesis 3:15, the Jews were the family through whom the Savior of the world was to be born. This one was promised to reverse the consequences of the failure in Eden, and as a result, bring blessing upon all the nations of the earth. If Israel, the *medium* of that promise, was disqualified, God's Genesis promise concerning the seed of Eve would be unfulfilled and his word invalidated. The adversary would have won the case leaving not only Joshua and his people without hope, but the whole human race as well. However, the adversary failed to take into account one vital aspect of the "case" – *the sovereignty of God.*

Joshua stood helplessly before YHWH with the accuser at his right hand (at the left-hand of God's throne) and the Angel of the Lord to the right of the throne. In that moment, we are given a window into heaven to observe one of the most remarkable transactions in all of redemptive history. The Lord of heaven and earth - the unbound God of freedom - *confronted and silenced the accuser with a verbal rebuke* through the mouth of his angel-advocate. He had chosen to justify his high priest, and by extension, the remnant of his people on the basis of nothing other than his own sovereign prerogative. YHWH declared that he plucked Joshua *out of the fire* (of consuming judgment) solely on the basis of his own good pleasure. He had no need of temple accoutrements, courtyard basins, lavers, or special mixtures of oil. He was not bound by the requirement for bulls, goats, rams, unleavened bread, cakes, pigeons, and turtledoves. This was meant to be a crucial lesson for the nation of Israel. Going forward, if they were to be a light to the nations, it would be necessary for them to understand the basis for their place in God's economy. It was not on the merits of their meticulous attention to rites and rituals – or because they had some particularly admirable qualities. From the very first call of God to their forefather Abraham down to the present, they had been privileged recipients of the sovereign grace of the living God, who had chosen to act favorably toward them. They were to understand that, in and of themselves, they had no inherent righteousness, deserved no special treatment, and their existence as a nation was solely dependent upon and sustained by his grace. That grace had placed them judicially in right standing before their God, as witnessed by the vision of this prophet.

Although there are differences of opinion as to the correct interpretation, many are convinced that this scene is referenced in the New Testament, in the Epistle of Jude:

> But Michael the archangel, when he disputed with the devil and argued about the body of Moses, did not dare pronounce against him a railing judgment, but said, "The Lord rebuke you!" (Jude 1:9).

Jude reflects upon this courtroom drama on display in our text. What irony that Satan, *the enemy* of all that is just and good, would dare to take up an argument with God about *justice*; standing before him and disputing that God, in the absence of the temple cleansing ritual, had no *legal right* to justify and preserve the nation. They failed in their obligation under the law, and from the accuser's point of view there was no blood sacrifice available to them because the whole temple system was in ruin.

The defense and the prosecutor came face-to-face, and Joshua was the defendant, but there was more at stake than simply Joshua *alone*.

Jude has shown us that the subject of the drama was God's right to justify the *body of Moses*. The body concerning which Jude wrote was not the *physical* body of the *man* Moses but the *body of the post-exilic Jewish remnant* preserved by the sovereign grace of God. It had to be preserved in order to perpetuate the purpose of God through the holy seed. Just as there now is a *body of Christ*, in the Old Testament there was a *body of Moses*. In 1 Corinthians 10:1-2, the Apostle Paul told the church that the nation of Israel was, "baptized into Moses in the cloud and in the sea" (i.e. the crossing of the Red Sea). This indicates that the people of Israel who made up the first covenant were the body of Moses, just as we who are baptized into Christ are the body of Christ, "For all of you who were baptized into Christ have *clothed yourselves with Christ*" (Galatians 3:27). The Old Testament Church was the body of God's people *clothed with* (or under the jurisdiction of) the law and economy of Moses.

REINSTITUTE AND CHARGE TO JOSHUA

Although the discussion is outside of the scope of this book, it is a common view among expositors that Zechariah was from a priestly family. It would be natural for him to make sure that the Lord did not forget to adorn Joshua with the clothing necessary for his service as the high priest. So, in the middle of this awesome event, the prophet chimes in with his own reminder to the heavenly throng, "Don't forget the turban!" He was definitely concerned that no detail be overlooked in this most important scene:

> Then I said, "Let them put a clean turban on his head." So they put a clean turban on his head and clothed him with garments, while the angel of the LORD was standing by. And the angel of the LORD admonished Joshua, saying, "Thus says the LORD of hosts, 'If you will walk in My ways and if you will perform My service, then you will also govern My house and also have charge of My courts, and I will grant you free access among these who are standing here'" (Zechariah 3:5-7).

Verses five and six again return us to the ordination ceremony in Exodus 29:

> You shall take the garments, and put on Aaron the tunic and the robe of the ephod and the ephod and the breastpiece, and gird him with the skillfully woven band of the ephod; and you shall set the turban on his head and put the holy crown on the turban (Exodus 29:5-6).

The excitement of Zechariah is best understood and appreciated when we contemplate the closing words of the consecration ceremony:

> I will meet there with the sons of Israel, and *it shall be consecrated by my glory.* I will consecrate the tent of meeting and the altar; I will also consecrate Aaron and his sons to minister as priests to me. *I will dwell among the sons of Israel and will be their God.* They shall know that I am the LORD their God who brought them out of the land of Egypt, that I might dwell among them; I am the LORD their God (Exodus 29:43-46).

The reinvestiture of the high priest could only mean one thing to the prophet; *God was preparing for His glory to return and dwell among His people.* Heaven, which had been uprooted from the earth for almost two generations, was about to be replanted. Gordon Fee explains:

> Central to the prophetic hope was the promised return of God's presence. Through Ezekiel, for example, God promises, "My dwelling place will be with them; I will be their God and they will be my people" (37:27); and Malachi prophesies, "Then suddenly the Lord you are seeking will come to his temple" (3:1) (Fee 1996:13).

Zechariah's interest in the turban is especially enlightening due to the fact that it was crowned with a tiara containing the words *Holy to the LORD* (Exodus 28:36-37). The high priest and representative of the nation had just been newly clothed with the "robe of righteousness" (Isaiah 61:10) symbolic of a fully redeemed man. It would appear that Zechariah wanted to make sure Joshua would be *reminded continuously* of his high calling as the tiara dangled about his head. YHWH then charged Joshua to be mindful of his privileged place of ministry before his presence on behalf of the people. YHWH also assured him that if he remained faithful, he would be granted perpetual access to the throne of grace. Verse seven establishes that this access to the *Holy of Holies* on the *Day of Atonement* on behalf of the people of God is viewed as nothing less than standing in the very presence of the heavenly council in the courtroom of YHWH.

To this point, the vision is powerful, but incomplete. Even though God's sovereign prerogative is an adequate basis for grace, the texts that follow bring us to the *literary center of the visionary experience*, where God discloses the basis upon which his grace can be so freely given.

MY SERVANT THE BRANCH

"Now listen, Joshua the high priest, you and your friends who are sitting in front of you--indeed they are men who are a symbol, for behold, I am going to bring in My servant the Branch. For behold, the stone that I have set before Joshua; on one stone are seven eyes. Behold, I will engrave an inscription on it," declares the LORD of hosts, "and I will remove the iniquity of that land in one day. In that day," declares the LORD of hosts, "every one of you will invite his neighbor to sit under his vine and under his fig tree" (Zechariah 3:8-10).

How little we realize our place in God. It is not likely that Joshua stood *physically* before the throne of the Lord, yet YHWH spoke in the hearing and seeing of Zechariah as if that were the case. The prophet may have been given this prophetic oracle at a time when Joshua was presiding over a general session of the council of priests (Kline

2001:119-120). However, from God's *eternal* vantage point, Joshua was standing *before him*, just as we, as a kingdom of priests, are now before the presence of the Lord having access through the blood of Christ. Where Joshua was on *earth* was secondary to the reality that he was a *heavenly man* positioned before the unseen God, a positional reality that Paul points out to the Ephesians:

> . . . even when we were dead in our transgressions, [God] made us alive together with Christ (by grace you have been saved), *and raised us up with Him, and seated us with Him in the heavenly places in Christ Jesus*. . . (Ephesians 2:5-6).

The Lord then stated that they, the priesthood, were but a symbol (or type) of the one who was to come. Of course, the one of whom he spoke is the *Lord Jesus Christ*, who is our great high priest. This is one of the amazing examples of the Bible's own self-witness to the *typological* nature of the Old Testament. The Lord made an unmistakably clear statement as to the *symbolic* nature of the priesthood - that it was representative of something greater yet to come (Hebrews 8:1-2).

In Zechariah 3:8-9, four prophetic symbols converge in this remarkable text: the *Servant*, the *Branch*, the *stone*, and the *eyes*. The terms *My Servant* and *The Branch* are both pregnant with meaning in the writings of the former prophets, especially those of Isaiah and Jeremiah. With regard to *the Servant of the Lord*, Isaiah 40-55 speaks extensively of him in four major passages (or *sections*). These are commonly referred to as the *Servant Songs*, and speak of the person and work of the Lord Jesus. The Servant of the Lord would:

- bear upon himself the Spirit of the Lord, and bring justice, light, and freedom from oppression to the nations (Isaiah 42:1-9).

- bear the glory of the Lord, restore the preserved ones of Israel, and be a light to the nations, bringing salvation to the ends of the earth (Isaiah 49:1-13).

- be obedient to the will of God and succeed in what he is sent to do by submitting to the abusive treatment of those who know not God (Isaiah 50:4-9).

- be exalted, but not until he bears the sting of death as the sin-bearer – the justifier of the many (Isaiah 52:13-53:12).

The *Servant* is but one aspect of this one to come. He is also the *Branch*. As the Branch of the Lord, he is the King from the line of David as spoken through Jeremiah:

> "Behold, the days are coming," declares the LORD,
> "When I will raise up for David a righteous Branch;
> And He will reign as king and act wisely
> And do justice and righteousness in the land.
> In His days Judah will be saved,
> And Israel will dwell securely;
> And this is His name by which He will be called,
> 'The LORD our righteousness'" (Jeremiah 23:5-6; cf. Jeremiah 33:15-16).

In Zechariah 3:9, the stone is the kingdom of the Messiah, Jesus, who himself is the *living stone* (1 Peter 2:4) prophesied by Daniel as he interpreted the dream of Nebuchadnezzar, king of Babylon:

> In the days of those kings the God of heaven will set up a kingdom which will never be destroyed, and that kingdom will not be left for another people; it will crush and put an end to all these kingdoms, but it will itself endure forever. Inasmuch as you saw that *a stone was cut out of the mountain without hands* and that it crushed the iron, the bronze, the clay, the silver and the gold, the great God has made known to the king what will take place in the future; so the dream is true and its interpretation is trustworthy (Daniel 2:44-45).

The *eyes*, as we learn later in the *Book of Revelation*, are the seven-fold Spirit of God who rests upon the Lord Jesus, as prophesied beforehand by Isaiah:

And I saw between the throne (with the four living creatures) and the elders a Lamb standing, as if slain, having seven horns and seven eyes, which are the seven Spirits of God, sent out into all the earth (Revelation 5:6).

Then a shoot will spring from the stem of Jesse, and a branch from his roots will bear fruit. The Spirit of the LORD will rest on Him, The spirit of wisdom and understanding, The spirit of counsel and strength, The spirit of knowledge and the fear of the LORD (Isaiah 11:1-2).

Finally, Joshua was told that this servant-king, who is also the stone that will crush all kingdoms, whose mountain will fill the whole earth, and upon whom the Spirit of the Lord rests - would also be *the one through whom YHWH would remove the iniquity of the land in a single moment in time.*

This passage looked forward to the day when, by a single act of divine power, God would break the dominion of iniquity and death from over his people, and their sins would be removed forever. There would no longer be a need for the arduous sacrificial system that demanded the blood of slaughtered bulls and goats to atone for the sins of the people. God would decisively accomplish this once and for all *in a single day* through the blood of his son, dealing the decisive death-blow at the cross of Jesus. The event is described to the letter of Zechariah's prophetic oracle − by the writer of the New Testament Letter to the Hebrews who affirms the finality of Jesus' once and for all sacrifice:

For it was fitting for us to have such a high priest, holy, innocent, undefiled, separated from sinners and exalted above the heavens; who does not need daily, like those high priests, to offer up sacrifices, first for His own sins and then for the sins of the people, *because this He did once for all when He offered up Himself* (Hebrews 7:26-27).

...then He said, "BEHOLD, I HAVE COME TO DO YOUR WILL." He takes away the first [covenant] in order to establish the second.

By this will *we have been sanctified through the offering of the body of Jesus Christ once for all* (Hebrews 10:9-10).

THE CENTRALITY OF JESUS CHRIST

If there is to be any true understanding of the nature of these visions with respect to the theme of *redefinition and enlargement*, it must be seen through the lens of the centrality of the Lord Jesus Christ. The indisputable literary and geographical center of Zechariah's visionary journey can be nothing other than the one who is the center of the whole purpose of God. As discussed earlier, the center of a literary chiasm marks *the key turning point or transition* in the poem or narrative. The utterance of the prophecy concerning the Lord Jesus promised the transition from sin to grace for the nation, and established her *true place* in redemptive history.

Walter Brueggemann articulates the essential meaning of the entire Old Testament story as follows:

> This list of books thus became the normative starting point and literary deposit from which arises the endless process of tradition and imagination whereby the community of Judaism is constituted and, derivatively, whereby the Christian community is given the resources through which to understand, affirm, and receive Jesus of Nazareth as the defining theological reality (Brueggemann 2003:6).

Israel's true definition as a nation under God could not be made any clearer than it is in our text under consideration. Her entire priestly ministry was instituted to be a *prophetic sign*, or literally, *men of a symbol* (Kline 2001:119) pointing forward to the true chosen priest of YHWH. The nation's entire existence, her entire literary corpus, and her entire temple ministry existed to light the way for God to be manifested in the flesh in Christ Jesus. Through Israel's own death (exile) and resurrection (release from Babylon), the world was being prepared for the gospel as the Old Testament people of God were being spread out into every nation under heaven to plant communities of faith, bringing with them the story and teachings of the one true God.

The narrative's closing verse (v. 10) projects an image of the Church living in peace and security (figuratively: *under the vine and fig tree*), but not in an exclusive manner. The people of God have become a relational people who now "invite his neighbor" to share along with them the blessings of the gospel. This *inclusionary* dimension is in contrast to a previous biblical description of the community of faith living in peace and security:

> So Judah and Israel lived in safety, every man under his vine and his fig tree, from Dan even to Beersheba, all the days of Solomon (1 Kings 4:25).

Under the *royal consciousness* of Solomon's economy (discussed Chapter 1) everyone secures *their own* vine and fig tree, to enjoy personal peace and prosperity. However, in the reconstituted post-exilic community of faith, there is a return to the *prophetic consciousness*, where, characteristically, the blessed ones *invite others to share* together the blessings (material and spiritual) of people of God. This capacity to reach out and share the grace which has been so freely given became the foundation for Zechariah's fifth vision, which continues in the temple complex.

THE RECONFIGURED LAMPSTAND

In conjunction with the foregoing revelation of Israel's role as witness to the nations, the prophet was awakened by the angel from his apparent sleep and discovered he had been moved out of the innermost sanctuary (the Holy of Holies) to the Holy Place of the temple where the golden lampstand, the table of showbread, and the altar of incense were located. The focal point of the vision was the lampstand. In Chapter 4 of Zechariah, the prophet was passing through the central transition point of the literary chiasm and was moving on an outbound path away from it, but was still in the temple proper.

> Then the angel who was speaking with me returned and roused me, as a man who is awakened from his sleep. He said to me, "What do you see?" And I said, "I see, and behold, a lampstand all of gold with its bowl on the top of it, and its seven lamps on it with seven spouts belonging to each of the lamps which are on the top of it; also two olive trees by it, one on the right side of the bowl and the other on its left side." Then I said to the angel who was speaking with me saying, "What are these, my lord?" So the angel who was speaking with me answered and said to me, "Do you not know what these are?" And I said, "No, my lord." Then he said to me, "This is the word of the LORD to Zerubbabel saying, 'Not by might nor by power, but by My Spirit,'" says the LORD of hosts (Zechariah 4:1-6).

When questioned by the angel, the prophet responded that he saw a particular furnishing in the Holy Place. A *menorah* or candlestick was not an unfamiliar sight in Zechariah's world, and although he may never have seen the original one inside of the Holy Place, he was undoubtedly familiar with the writings of Moses and the particular menorah that was maintained within the house of God. However, there was something odd about *this* candlestick. Although it is difficult to precisely interpret Zechariah's description, it appears that this candlestick was *seven times brighter* than the one built by Moses. Each of the original seven branches seems to have had additional lamps around them:

> The picture is of seven small bowls, each with a place for seven wicks, arranged round the rim of the main bowl . . . With its *seven times seven lights* it would be both impressive and effective (Baldwin 1972:120).

> Each of the seven lamps is itself of the seven with design . . . Giving *a total of forty-nine lamp lights* (Kline 2001:132).

The lampstand was post-exilic Israel, and the flame that she bore was the knowledge of YHWH. In a New Testament context, the same symbol is used to describe the *churches* in the *Book of Revelation* where John saw the ascended Christ *walking among the candlesticks*.

> Then I turned to see the voice that was speaking with me. And having turned I saw seven golden lampstands; and *in the middle of the lampstands I saw one like a son of man*, clothed in a robe reaching to the feet, and girded across His chest with a golden sash… "As for the mystery of the seven stars which you saw in My right hand, and the seven golden lampstands: the seven stars are the angels of the seven churches, *and the seven lampstands are the seven churches*" (Revelation 1:12-13, 20).

Throughout the history of the tabernacle of Moses, the light of God was kept burning 24 hours a day, seven days a week *by the priesthood*. However, in this vision there are other sources feeding the lamps. The prophet saw two olive trees providing a constant supply of oil to keep the menorah burning as described in verse twelve. In response to the prophet's question, the angel went on to explain that it is not by human agency, effort, military power, or strength that the knowledge of God is being sustained in Israel and the world. Nor is it the priesthood who keeps the lamps trimmed, supplied, and burning, but *YHWH alone* who is the supplier of all that is needed to sustain and promulgate the knowledge of himself in the world. The agency through which he accomplishes this is none other than the presence and power of his Spirit.

The image of the seven flames which characterized the light of God in the Mosaic tabernacle was being *redefined* to suit a new context and *enlarged* to accommodate the now global presence of God's people. The people of God are the light of God in the world, as they are bearers of his presence through the Spirit.

> "*You* are the light of the world. A city set on a hill cannot be hidden" (Matthew 5:14).

This new reality was prophesied by Isaiah in highly symbolic language almost two centuries earlier. Rather than the *menorah*, Isaiah uses the *brightness of the sun* as a metaphor to describe the same post-exilic reality (it is not unusual for biblical authors to use different metaphors to describe the same truth):

> The light of the moon will be as the light of the sun, and *the light of the sun will be seven times brighter, like the light of seven days*, on the day the LORD binds up the fracture of His people and heals the bruise He has inflicted (Isaiah 30:26).

The light borne by the people of God is the knowledge of God introduced to all the nations as his plan and purpose was being sustained and perpetuated by the Holy Spirit. It is not Israel or the Church that sustain the knowledge of God in the world, but God himself who sustains his own testimony in and through his people. This would come about in Israel, according to Isaiah, as a result of the return from exile.

GRACE! GRACE!

What followed was a great oracle of affirmation and the expression of the Spirit's delight as Zerubbabel, the Governor of Judah, would build the house of God in the face of enemy opposition. Zerubbabel was assured that he would accomplish this, not by human strength or military force, but by the impetus of the Holy Spirit of God. The Spirit had been sent to assure completion of the work.

> What are you, O great mountain? Before Zerubbabel you will become a plain; and he will bring forth the top stone with shouts of "Grace, grace to it!" Also the word of the LORD came to me, saying, "The hands of Zerubbabel have laid the foundation of this house, and his hands will finish it. Then you will know that the LORD of hosts has sent me to you. For who has despised the day of small

things? But these seven will be glad when they see the plumb line in the hand of Zerubbabel - these are the eyes of the LORD which range to and fro throughout the earth." Then I said to him, "What are these two olive trees on the right of the lampstand and on its left?" And I answered the second time and said to him, "What are the two olive branches which are beside the two golden pipes, which empty the golden oil from themselves?" So he answered me, saying, "Do you not know what these are?" And I said, "No, my lord." Then he said, "These are the two anointed ones who are standing by the Lord of the whole earth" (Zechariah 4:7-14).

Again the context shifted to a victory cry from the mouth of the angel. The recipient of his exhortation was the federal head of the nation, Zerubbabel, the governor of Judah. The angel assured Zerubbabel that in spite of whatever great obstacles were before him (political, military, or other), God's unalterable purpose would be fulfilled, and before him, the seemingly insurmountable obstacles (the great mountain) would fall. Zerubbabel was assured that he would accomplish the rebuilding of the house of God, and that its capstone would be set in place amid exuberant shouts from among his people. The cap or top stone is most likely a metaphor for completing the work. It is the final stone which completes the structure. He was not to be concerned with the opposition from foreign forces or the apparent humble beginnings of this restoration community and its efforts. The Spirit of the Lord would be pleased as he prepared to build. The people of God would witness the completion of the task - rejoicing with exuberant shouts, and the lamp of God would never go out because it was being sustained and perpetuated by divine resources.

CONTEMPORARY RELEVANCE

The entire sanctuary experience of Zechariah is one grand view of the *transition from sin to grace*, the promise of Jesus the Servant-Branch,

and the emanation of the light of God through his redefined candlestick - the remnant of Israel.

1. Zechariah's vision of Joshua the high priest is an extraordinary
examination of sinful man before his God. Man stands before him covered in filth, hopeless, without a single fiber of righteousness by which
to justify himself before God's throne. It is *grace and grace alone* - the
exercise of divine prerogative - that causes God to silence the accuser,
strip the sinner of his filthy garments, and re-clothe him with garments
of praise, righteousness, and service. However, a most notable detail in
this vision is not that it involves the *lost sinner*, but that it is the *people of
God* who must be *reoriented to grace*. In this vision, we, like the nation of
Israel, must be fundamentally stripped of all self-righteousness which
like a cancer, erodes our Christian witness. The context of this entire
transitional vision is the *emanating light of witness* of the people of God.
Only when our own hearts are deeply convicted with the knowledge of
our own sinfulness and the unfathomable magnitude of God's grace
upon our own lives, can we truly reach out to others with authentic
missional humility. How often do we succumb to the temptation to look
down others, unwittingly acting as though we *deserve* the place we have
in God, or that somehow we made a "choice" to serve him. Our role
within the culture we live is one of ambassadorship, through which we
make a heartfelt *appeal* for others to be reconciled to God through the
cross of his Son, by which we ourselves have also been reconciled as a
result of his unfathomable grace.

> Therefore if anyone is in Christ, he is a new creature; the old things
> passed away; behold, new things have come. Now all these things
> are from God, who reconciled us to Himself through Christ and
> gave us the ministry of reconciliation, namely, that God was in Christ
> reconciling the world to Himself, not counting their trespasses
> against them, and He has committed to us the word of reconcilia-
> tion. Therefore, we are ambassadors for Christ, as though God were
> making an appeal through us; we beg you on behalf of Christ, be
> reconciled to God. He made Him who knew no sin to be sin on our

behalf, so that we might become the righteousness of God in Him (2 Corinthians 5: 17-21).

Just as the humility of the Servant and the dominion of the Branch are perfectly merged together in Jesus, so also must they be in us. The oracle concerning the Lord Jesus in Zechariah 3 foresees the great poem of the apostle Paul in his letter to the Philippians:

> Have this attitude in yourselves which was also in Christ Jesus, who, although He existed in the form of God, did not regard equality with God a thing to be grasped, but emptied Himself, taking the form of a bond-servant, and being made in the likeness of men. Being found in appearance as a man, He humbled Himself by becoming obedient to the point of death, even death on a cross. For this reason also, God highly exalted Him, and bestowed on Him the name which is above every name, so that at the name of Jesus EVERY KNEE WILL BOW, of those who are in heaven and on earth and under the earth, and that every tongue will confess that Jesus Christ is Lord, to the glory of God the Father (Philippians 2:5-11).

The apostle is not inviting us to pray, "Lord empty me of myself," but exhorting us to *make a conscious choice of emptying ourselves* each day before the Lord on behalf of others. Each time we choose to humble ourselves when we have a right to be angry, frustrated, critical, or self-serving, we are touching the servant-heart of Jesus. This calls for blessing and forgiving when we have been wronged, trusting fully in God when circumstances are against us, and saying no to sin when it is "crouching at the door" (Genesis 4:7). When we, like Jesus, take the form of a bond-servant, then and only then are we on the path to true victory and reigning with him in life.

2. The candlestick experience of Zechariah illustrates what actually transpires once we have passed through the *crisis of reorientation*. In the aftermath of its crisis, the humbled and vulnerable nation – in spite of having few resources, no central military force, no earthly king, and

scattered among all the nations – had now become the *light of the world*. Having watched the walls of her former world come crumbling down at the violent hand of an oppressive nation, little could she imagine that she was being borne along by the God of all grace to be the instrument through which the knowledge of YHWH would be spread beyond the borders of Israel – in spite of her sins, her failures, and her idolatries.

We simply cannot conceive the potential for influence when God takes us through the process of *redefinition and enlargement* through crisis. When it seems that the walls of our world are crumbling and unspeakable pain has entered our lives, we (as families or communities) are but *candlesticks* being re-shaped, re-formed, and given a supply of oil that comes not from man but from God himself. Our lamp will ultimately *burn with seven times the brightness* of its former state.

My own personal crisis resulted in the capability to relate to people in ways that I never thought possible had I not experienced the humiliation and the loss through which God brought me. Seven times, among other things, means we are now enlarged to share the knowledge of God into a broader variety of environments and a greater variety of peoples, cultures, and worldviews. In my professional world, and even in my former ministerial world of the 1970s, there unwittingly existed a kind of condescension toward those who were different or less fortunate. Through the exile, I was forced to stand face-to-face with God to see my own capacity for evil, and bow down before him realizing I was as nothing before him.

3. The candlestick vision means, at least in part, that the grace *received* in Zechariah 3 was given to be *released* as seen in Zechariah 4. Just as the destroying mountain, those powers which were obstacles to the building would be brought down, so also our own obstacles of bitterness, unforgiveness, anger, criticism, and self-righteousness are leveled as the grace that has been received in our hearts is released. The shouts of grace in the visions seen by the prophet arose out of what abided within:

The good man out of the good treasure of his heart brings forth what is good; and the evil man out of the evil treasure brings forth what is evil; for his mouth speaks from that which fills his heart (Luke. 6:45).

As we have freely received, we must freely give, not begrudgingly, but with "shouts" of exuberant joy - inasmuch as we have been freely given his grace, we freely and joyfully release grace to others. This demands a radical transformation of the inner man, but as we yield, we will release our own hearts from the ungodly powers of hurt, resentment, self-righteousness, and the critical spirit that seeks to bring us under its control. The destroying mountain was no match for men and women filled with the Spirit of life declaring grace over others, over their place of worship, over their families, over those who had wounded them, over their enemies, over their leaders, over their parents, and over their children. In order to truly be the light of the world that shines seven times brighter, the recipients of the unfathomable grace of God must become the channels of that same grace. Grace is given to the community of faith, in order that it might be assimilated into the culture of the Church and released to others. This was inherent within the very first encounter between God and Abraham, where Abraham was told:

"I will bless you . . . and you shall be a blessing. . ." (Genesis 12:2).

4. The two olive trees that feed the lampstand (which in turn keeps the lamp of God burning among his people) may be seen as the restoration of the balance of power and testimony between the priesthood and the kingdom. The priesthood represents the *liturgical* aspects of the community of faith such as worship, Bible study, and the Lord's Supper. The kingdom represents the *public or social* aspect of the community, such as doing good works, ensuring justice and healing for the oppressed, and feeding the poor - those things that are typically

done outside of the Church's regular liturgical practice. The oil of the Spirit feeds the lamp of God in the Church and shines brightest when both dimensions are expressed in a balanced manner. If we focus only on worship and prayer meetings, we may edify *ourselves*, but risk losing touch with the community around us. The opposite is also true. If we engage in social actions without strong prayer and worship to cover and empower our activities, we become little more than a social agency, and possibly risk burn-out. For Israel, it meant the reversal of centuries of subjection of their priesthood to interests of the state. That arrangement produced scores of false prophets like those in Jeremiah's day who kept promising their corrupt kings that God would deliver them from Babylon. Obviously, they were wrong.

Chapter 6

THE SIXTH VISION
THE FLYING SCROLL

The visionary scenes of the prophet continue on their outbound trajectory away from the central sanctuary and back to the holy city and the land. Zechariah saw a large flying scroll approximately 30 feet by 15 feet - based on the biblical cubit which was about 18 inches - with writing on both sides. The vision was followed by a dialogue with his host angel.

> Then I lifted up my eyes again and looked, and behold, there was a flying scroll. And he said to me, "What do you see?" And I answered, "I see a flying scroll; its length is twenty cubits and its width ten cubits." Then he said to me, "This is the curse that is going forth over the face of the whole land; surely everyone who steals will be purged away according to the writing on one side, and everyone who swears will be purged away according to the writing on the other side. I will make it go forth," declares the LORD of hosts, "and it will enter the house of the thief and the house of the one who swears falsely by My name; and it will spend the night within that house and consume it with its timber and stones" (Zechariah 5:1-4).

THE SCROLL

The scroll in this vision immediately brings to mind the law of God as it hovered over the whole land as a testimony to Israel's original covenant arrangements given at Mount Sinai. It was referred to by the angel as a *curse*, which among the ancients was synonymous with *oath* or *covenant*. This is largely due to the fact that covenants contained both blessings for the loyal and curses or sanctions for those who were disloyal or disobedient to its stipulations. The law imagery is further suggested by the writing found on *both sides*, which is also said of the stone tablets given at Mount Sinai:

> Then Moses turned and went down from the mountain with the two tablets of the testimony in his hand, tablets *which were written on both sides;* they were written on one side and the other (Exodus 32:15).

The vision identified the sin of *stealing* from one side of the scroll and *swearing falsely* (probably arrogant oath-making or assertion of personal innocence) on the other, as of particular interest to God. The writing on both sides implies its comprehensiveness, including responsibilities to both God and man. The third commandment of the first tablet forbids swearing falsely in his name as a *duty to God*. The forbidding of theft, according to the eighth commandment and recorded on the second tablet, is a duty to one's neighbor. This is a commonly held view among commentators. It is not likely that these are the only issues God had with his people, and it is therefore reasonable to assume that a literary device may be in use in Zechariah's description. The device is called *synecdoche* (pronounced: sin-ek-do-kee), which is *the use of a sample as a reflection of the whole*. The former prophets, when calling Israel to task for their sins, often identified a sample such as Sabbath breaking, immorality, civic injustice, or idolatry to reflect that the nation was guilty of the whole law.

THE "PURGING AWAY"

God's method of dealing with these issues was, as the prophet points out, to *enter the house as a consuming fire, spending the night until all is consumed*. Again we find in the New Testament an equivalent from the mouth of John the Baptist:

John answered and said to them all, "As for me, I baptize you with water; but One is coming who is mightier than I, and I am not fit to untie the thong of His sandals; He will baptize you with the Holy Spirit and fire" (Luke 3:16).

In Zechariah 5:3, the translation of the Hebrew text as "purged away" in the *NASB*, and similarly in many translations, seems to suggest the *removal, condemnation,* or *destruction* of the sinning parties. However, both *Strong's Concordance* and the *Theological Wordbook the Old Testament* suggest an interpretation of the word which has an interestingly redemptive sense:

> A primitive root; to be (or make) clean (literally or figuratively); by implication (in an adverse sense) to be bare, that is, extirpated: - (Strong's #H5352).

> Otherwise the word evokes favorable connotations. It may be used to denote *freedom from an oath.* (Genesis 24:8; Joshua 2:17, 20). . . This tends to reinforce the analysis: "poured out, emptied" yields "*be freed, cleared, cleansed, innocent.*" ... A political use of this word, namely, freedom or exemption from some obligation such as military service (Deuteronomy 24:5) serves to sharpen its forensic [legal; judicial] sense of being *freed from punishment* (Harris, Archer, Waltke 1980:596-597).

The sense of freedom from the curse is captured in *Young's Literal Translation*:

> And he saith unto me, "This is the execration [curse] that is going forth over the face of all the land, for every one who is stealing, on the one side, according to it, *hath been declared innocent,* and every one who hath sworn, on the other side, according to it, *hath been declared innocent.* I have brought it out--an affirmation of Jehovah of Hosts--and it hath come in unto the house of the thief, and unto

the house of him who hath sworn in My name to a falsehood, and it hath remained in the midst of his house, and hath consumed it, both its wood and its stones" (Zechariah. 5:3-4).

Fred P. Miller offers this excellent analysis:

"Cut off." Hebrew "niqqah," is a passive verb which means to be cleansed or purified. Most translations (ASV, KJV, and NIV) and commentaries consistently follow the idea of removing of the guilty parties through punishment. However the literal meaning in the words is that the content of the roll will cleanse and purify the sinner. This is the direct meaning of the passage while the context speaks of removing the houses, timber, and all. The context may have led the commentators to use the secondary meaning of the word, that is, the sinners are to be cleaned out, removed, or as they say "cut off" from the land. The more natural meaning of the passage which is consistent with the grammar and vocabulary used is: "The words on one side of the scroll will cleanse the liar when he compares himself to it and the words on the other side of the scroll will cleanse the thief when he compares himself to it" (Miller 1999).

BEHAVIOR MATTERS

This vision, along with the one that follows, deal with the issue of judgment *within the covenant realm* (Kline 2001:177). Both are concerned with unholy elements that remain among the now justified people of God. That is to say, that in as much as Israel had been cleansed *judicially* by the sovereign grace of God as we observed in Zechariah 4, she needed to understand that her *practical behavior* was still of concern to God. Both the Old and New Testaments clearly indicate his testimony to the world is not *only* the verbal declaration of his saving power, but also its authentication by the good works and exemplary living of those who call upon his name. The community of faith as a visible model of his reconciling and sanctifying power before the world at large is emphasized in both the Old and New Testaments:

See, I have taught you statutes and judgments just as the LORD my God commanded me, that you should do thus in the land where you are entering to possess it. So keep and do them, for that is your wisdom and your understanding in the sight of the peoples who will hear all these statutes and say, "Surely this great nation is a wise and understanding people" (Deuteronomy 4:5-6).

You are the light of the world. A city set on a hill cannot be hidden; nor does anyone light a lamp and put it under a basket, but on the lampstand, and it gives light to all who are in the house. Let your light shine before men in such a way that they may see your good works, and glorify your Father who is in heaven (Matthew 5:14-16).

These texts describing the exemplary role of God's people are essentially equivalent, one from the Old Testament, and one from the New. Without demeaning the primary importance of saving faith, note the emphasis of both Moses and the Lord Jesus upon the *collective behavior* of the people of God as a witness to God's saving grace. The verbal testimony declared by the Church must be undergirded by appropriate behavior and accompanying lifestyle which characterize a community *demonstrating the presence of God's reign as well as his salvation from sin.* We cannot hide behind statements such as, "Don't look at me, just look at Jesus." If the dying world is going to see Jesus, they're going to see him in *us.* The Holy Spirit's presence in the Church is, among other things, to transform us into the image and character of the Lord Jesus and to manifest through mortal flesh the presence of his eternal, heavenly kingdom.

YHWH's restorative grace was vividly portrayed in the previous two visions reminding Israel from where she had come and the true nature of her condition apart from her God. In addition, the candlestick vision awakened to her the fact that the grace she had received was to be a light to the world around her and freely given in the same manner as it had been received. Here, Zechariah was presented a third aspect of her restoration, *a return to the covenantal obligations of the word of God*. As it was again given its proper place as the community's definitive literary volume, it served as the vehicle upon which the Holy Spirit's purging power would bring about practical holiness before God and in the eyes of the world.

The activity of this vision actually reflects a vision of Isaiah almost 200 years prior. Isaiah, in the great throne room vision of the Lord where he received his commission to prophesy, heard the Lord's statement that *his people's eyes would be dim and their ears dull of hearing*. The prophet asked, "How long?" - and was given the explanation that once the exile was completed the remnant (tenth) would necessarily be subject to *further purging*.

> Then I said, "Lord, how long?" And He answered, "Until cities are devastated and without inhabitant, Houses are without people and the land is utterly desolate, The LORD has removed men far away, and the forsaken places are many in the midst of the land [*a prophecy of the exile*]. Yet there will be a tenth portion in it, and *it will again be subject to burning*, like a terebinth or an oak whose stump remains when it is felled. The holy seed is its stump" (Isaiah 6:11-13).

Once the people of God had gone through their exile and returned to the land, Isaiah was told that there would be yet another *burning* that would further purge the remnant of his people, who were but the stump of what had once been a great tree. However, Isaiah is assured that the holy seed that would continue in his redemptive plan *would continue from within that stump*.

CONTEMPORARY RELEVANCE

1. There is a connection between this vision and Jesus' parable of *The Sower*, which speaks to the issue of the *internal*, personal issues that keep us from fully attaining to the purpose of God:

Hear then the parable of the sower. When anyone hears the word of the kingdom and does not understand it, the evil one comes and snatches away what has been sown in his heart. This is the one on whom seed was sown beside the road. The one on whom seed was sown on the rocky places, this is the man who hears the word and immediately receives it with joy; yet he has no firm root in himself, but is only temporary, and when affliction or persecution arises because of the word, immediately he falls away. And the one on whom seed was sown among the thorns, this is the man who hears the word, and the worry of the world and the deceitfulness of wealth choke the word, and it becomes unfruitful. And the one on whom seed was sown on the good soil, this is the man who hears the word and understands it; who indeed bears fruit and brings forth, some a hundredfold, some sixty, and some thirty (Matthew 13:18).

Jesus spoke of various conditions internal to people, none of which need be considered *irreversible*. Each of the recipients of the seed (the word of the kingdom) harbored internal conditions which served as the soil that either hindered or supported growth and fruitfulness. These conditions, or *internal hindrances* – are the very target of the Holy Spirit's purging process which is also suggested by Zechariah's vision. Interestingly, in Zechariah, the Holy Spirit's cleansing work is seen in a new context; it is *personalized in the life of the believer*, which indicates an individual, personal intimacy with YHWH. With the exception of the great men and women of faith, this is rarely, if ever heard of in the former writings of Moses and the prophets. Typically, the Old Testament writings speak of God's dealing with the nation as a whole, but here he is indicating to Zechariah that he knows each sheep by name, something that would come to be fully understood in the New Testament (cf. John 10:1-3).

2. *Grace is not license.* As the people of God, we have been called not only to enjoy the unspeakable privilege of right standing with God through the cross of Jesus, but also to bear the responsibility of a personal and community life that bears witness to both his holiness

and his conciliatory power. Just as Jesus promised that the reception of the Holy Spirit by the Church would empower us to be his witnesses throughout the world (Acts 1: 8), the Bible also promised that we would be baptized (immersed) in *the Holy Spirit and fire* (Luke 3:16). It is liberating to have been declared innocent by the grace of God, washed in the blood of Christ, and having right standing before him solely and exclusively on that basis. However, God is not blind to the weaknesses of our flesh and that there is further work to be done. The night is often long and painful indeed during which God "visits our house" (Zechariah 5:4) - baptizing us in his consuming fire. He does so to expose our falsehood, strongholds of unbelief, greed, lust, self-interest, and pride - making them into ashes in order that we may bear the image of Christ.

The testimony of the people of God cannot merely be religious observance that does not have corresponding ethical outcomes. Observe the words of Jeremiah just prior to the Babylonian exile:

> The word that came to Jeremiah from the LORD, saying, "Stand in the gate of the LORD's house and proclaim there this word and say, 'Hear the word of the LORD, all you of Judah, who enter by these gates to worship the LORD!'" Thus says the LORD of hosts, the God of Israel, and "Amend your ways and your deeds, and I will let you dwell in this place. Do not trust in deceptive words, saying, 'This is the temple of the LORD, the temple of the LORD, the temple of the LORD.' For if you truly amend your ways and your deeds, if you truly practice justice between a man and his neighbor, if you do not oppress the alien, the orphan, or the widow, and do not shed innocent blood in this place, nor walk after other gods to your own ruin, then I will let you dwell in this place, in the land that I gave to your fathers forever and ever. Behold, you are trusting in deceptive words to no avail. Will you steal, murder, and commit adultery and swear falsely, and offer sacrifices to Baal and walk after other gods that you have not known, then come and stand before Me in this house, which is called by My name, and say, 'We are delivered!'- that

you may do all these abominations? Has this house, which is called by My name, become a den of robbers in your sight? Behold, I, even I, have seen it," declares the LORD (Jeremiah 7:1-11).

As was the case in ancient Israel, so it is today for the Church. "Temple" religion with its liturgical observance is, by itself, insufficient – it is only half of the community's *bios*, or *form of life* (Stone 2007:24-25). The people of God are *also* distinguished by their collective and personal behavior outside the church walls. The redefined city of God that we considered in Zechariah 2 had no *physical walls*, but that does not suggest that it had no *defining boundaries*. Everything that enters to abide there must pass through the *wall of fire* (Zechariah 2:5), which is the consuming judgment of God. The boundaries, therefore, are *ethical* in nature. In contrast to mere conformance to externals of the Pharisees, true holiness and godly love spring from a transformed inward person, making the people of God distinct by their character.

3. God is far more interested in our *character* than our *feelings*. We must embrace the often painful purging process as the means by which God, who always sees from the eternal perspective, accomplishes his desire in those who were called by his name. Those of us who live in North America are especially prone to cling to the notions of temporal well-being and prosperity as if they were God-given *rights* and therefore struggle with notions of pain and/or suffering. Some even consider it scandalous to suggest that it might come from the hand of God. We may likely confront God with questions like, "Why me?" or, "How much is enough?" This, of course, while all the time maintaining our outwardly pious veneer. This is not to suggest that the Father doesn't understand when we are hurt, lonely, or confused - he most certainly does; but he also has eternal purposes far beyond our capacity to comprehend. The formation of the character of his people into the image of Christ far outweighs our need for temporal well-being and security. When he challenges us to, "pick up your cross and follow me," he is not inviting us to *life, liberty, and the pursuit of happiness.* Yet, the same

time, he has assured us that regardless of what may befall us in this life, if we set our hearts to pursue the kingdom and his righteousness, we will not want for the basic necessities of life (Matthew 6:31-33).

4. This vision illustrates that not only is *justification* unattainable in and of ourselves, as was seen in Zechariah 3 (The Throne Room Vision), but the same is true for *sanctification*. It too is accomplished by means of the Holy Spirit's fire operating in the lives of his people. We may accomplish varying degrees of self-control over the outer man, which the Scriptures encourage, but this by itself amounts to essentially *law keeping or legalism*. This vision, however, reminds us that the underlying wickedness in the human heart can only be purged through the agency of God's Spirit. He will consume everything that is not compatible with his holiness. It therefore also discourages passivity in the life of the believer, bringing a balanced approach which encourages active pursuit of the Spirit of God for the exercise of his grace to cleanse our hearts, so that what flows out is a pure stream. That being said, we bear the responsibility of yielding to God's process in order be transformed by it. We can resist the purging work of the Spirit, of which both the Old and New Testaments testify:

> It is for discipline that you endure; God deals with you as with sons; for what son is there whom his father does not discipline? But if you are without discipline, of which all have become partakers, then you are illegitimate children and not sons. Furthermore, we had earthly fathers to discipline us, and we respected them; shall we not much rather be subject to the Father of spirits, and live? (Hebrews 12:7-9).

> Who among you will give ear to this? Who will give heed and listen hereafter? Who gave Jacob up for spoil, and Israel to plunderers? Was it not the LORD, against whom we have sinned, and in whose ways they were not willing to walk, and whose law they did not obey? So He poured out on him the heat of His anger and the fierceness of battle; and it set him aflame all around, *yet he did not recognize it; and it burned him, but he paid no attention* (Isaiah 42:23-25).

Such resistance only prolongs the pain. The more readily we recognize God as the source, see his purpose, and submit to his hand, the more quickly we will experience the ensuing "peaceable fruit of righteousness" (Hebrews 12:11).

5. The enduring effectiveness of God's Word was reinforced as Zechariah saw the personified word of God going throughout the land to seek out and purge impurities from God's household. The prophet's vision is of the ever-living, always relevant Word of God, exercising its creative power *900 years* from the time it was first uttered to the prophet Moses. Walter Wink has observed:

> One of the best ways to discern the weakness of a social system is to discover what it excludes from conversation (Wink 1986:1).

The people of God are weakened when the word of God ceases to be central to our lives and conversation. We lose the very vehicle upon which the Holy Spirit conveys to us relevant truth and wisdom, exposes our need, answers our deepest questions, and recalibrates our lives in alignment with his will. God always assures us that his message is never outdated, always ready to be re-articulated in new situations where his people need to hear his voice and experience its dynamic, life-changing power.

There are no shortcuts when it comes to God's accomplishing of the purging work in the life of the believer. When he comes "to spend the night," it is in order that he might transform the darkness in our hearts into the light of his holiness and love. It is a long and often unbearable night - a season of deep self-examination and revelation as we struggle to overcome condemnation and receive his cleansing and transforming grace.

Chapter 7

THE SEVENTH VISION
FILL UP THE MEASURE

The sixth and seventh visions deal with the removal of ungodliness from the covenant realm, which is to say, from among God's people. The previous vision characterized the purging of *internal hindrances* from the remnant. This next vision addresses the removal of *external hindrances*. Both this and the previous vision appear to have been located in the context of the cities of the land, and possibly Jerusalem. These two visions are being treated separately, although some have argued that the *scroll and ephah* are actually a single vision (Kline 2001:177). Whether or not it is the case, our lessons remain unaffected by that distinction.

> Then the angel who was speaking with me went out and said to me, "Lift up now your eyes and see what this is going forth." I said, "What is it?" And he said, "This is the ephah going forth." Again he said, "This is their appearance in all the land (and behold, a lead cover was lifted up); and this is a woman sitting inside the ephah." Then he said, "This is Wickedness!" And he threw her down into the middle of the ephah and cast the lead weight on its opening. Then I lifted up my eyes and looked, and there two women were coming out with the wind in their wings; and they had wings like the wings of a stork, and they lifted up the ephah between the earth and the heavens. I said to the angel who was speaking with me, "Where are they taking the ephah?" Then he said to me, "To build a temple for her in the land of Shinar; and when it is prepared, she will be set there on her own pedestal" (Zechariah 5:5-11).

THE EPHAH, THE LEAD WEIGHT, AND THE WOMAN

The host angel escorted Zechariah out from the city to the surrounding land. The prophet's eyes fell upon an *ephah* (approximately one bushel), within which a woman was being held. It is likely, although not specifically stated, that the bushel was of exaggerated dimensions in order to be able to hold her. The ephah was a fairly common household bushel, having the capacity of about 5-10 gallons (exact capacity is uncertain) and also used as a commercial standard of measure. It was typically used for measuring out grain (Ruth 2:17; 1 Samuel 1:24). The prophet Amos also used it as a symbol of injustice in commerce. He condemned merchants for anxiously waiting for the holy days to be completed so they could go back to the work of taking unfair advantage of others by using false measures:

> "Hear this, you who trample the needy, to do away with the humble of the land, saying, 'When will the new moon be over, So that we may sell grain, And the Sabbath, that we may open the wheat market, To make the bushel [Hebrew: *ephah*] smaller and the shekel bigger, And to cheat with dishonest scales'" (Amos 8:4-5).

The lead weight was actually a *talent-weight* used in the marketplace, estimated to be about 75 pounds (Kline 2001:185). It was commonly used as a counterbalance to weigh out silver and gold. The fair and just use of these two standards are mentioned in the law of Moses and the Proverbs:

> "You shall do no wrong in judgment, in measurement of weight, or capacity. You shall have just balances, just weights, a just ephah, and a just hin; I am the LORD your God, who brought you out from the land of Egypt" (Leviticus 19:35-36).

> "You shall not have in your bag differing weights, a large and a small. You shall not have in your house differing measures, a large and a small. You shall have a full and just weight; you shall have a full and

just measure, that your days may be prolonged in the land which the LORD your God gives you. For everyone who does these things, everyone who acts unjustly is an abomination to the LORD your God" (Deuteronomy 25:13-16).

Differing weights and differing measures, both of them are abominable to the LORD (Proverbs 20:10).

The marketplace, as it is today, was a normal and common part of life. In and of themselves, buying, selling, and bartering for goods and services were not inherently evil, but were to be governed by the law of God to be conducted in a fair and just manner. To act otherwise would infect the domestic relationships among Israelites with a spirit of greed, which was to have no place in God's economy. In the passage above from Leviticus 19, it is worthy of observation that the command for fairness in the marketplace is given on the basis that the Lord had brought them "out from the land of Egypt." In other words they were delivered from such practices of greed in pagan marketplaces to be radically and entirely holy unto God in all aspects of life. One of Israel's most sacred texts, the *Shema*, instructed God's people by the mouth of Moses to:

"Hear, O Israel! The LORD is our God, the LORD is one!" (Deuteronomy 6:4).

This meant, among other things, that they were not to live their life by one set of rules in the sanctuary and a separate set of rules in the various aspects of day-to-day living. The *one God* to whom they offered worship and sacrifice of the temple was the same God who ruled them in the marketplace. The practice of serving different gods in different environments may have been suitable for pagan nations who served various gods of various domains, but it had no place in YHWH's domain (see Frost 2003:127). Unfortunately, Israel had become accustomed to an economy of *Godless commercialism*. In spite of all that God had done for them in their history, their ancient tribal league's decision to "be like the nations" had matured into a fully-orbed culture of keeping religion to one side of life and the marketplace on the other, just like her pagan neighbors.

The woman most assuredly represents the *harlot spirit*, which pervaded Israelite culture. A woman so clearly identified and associated with *wickedness* would typically represent a harlot. She was also *hidden from view*, which required Zechariah's host angel to lift the cover to expose her. YHWH's people had no idea of the invisible forces that were influencing them. The angel also explained that this was, "Their appearance (Hebrew: *eye*) in all the land," indicating that this was not a *selective* purging of lawbreakers as in the previous vision, but the exposure of an ungodly cultural influence *that had permeated the whole of the remnant in the land*. The Hebrew *ayin*, translated *appearance* is also translated elsewhere to mean *fountain* or *spring* (Harris 1980:663). The analogy is intended to indicate that Israel's spring, or *source of life*, was not YHWH, but the spirit of commercialism. This source of life is a common metaphor in biblical language to describe the defining forces that shape and sustain us:

> "Be appalled, O heavens, at this, and shudder, be very desolate," declares the LORD. "For My people have committed two evils: They have forsaken Me, The fountain of living waters, to hew for themselves cisterns, Broken cisterns that can hold no water" (Jeremiah 2:12-13).

Jesus also used the metaphor in relationship to greed:

> But if your *eye* is bad, your whole body will be full of darkness. If then the light that is in you is darkness, how great is the darkness! No one can serve two masters; for either he will hate the one and love the other, or he will be devoted to one and despise the other. You cannot serve God and wealth [Mammon] (Matthew 6:23-24).

Both texts have in view sources of life other than YHWH. Jeremiah spoke to those who, in the face of crisis, sought refuge in Egypt as a sustaining source and the Lord Jesus who warned that commercialism (Mammon) competes with God for the ownership of the hearts of people. Try as we might, we cannot serve both – whether we refer to it as God and Egypt, or God and Mammon.

A NEW FORM OF IDOLATRY

We are told by the Scriptures that in the Exodus, when the children of Israel left Egypt to become God's own prize possession, they brought with them idols from their former life, and an idolatrous tabernacle in which they may have offered their children as sacrifices to other gods (specifically Moloch). Because of their unbelief, they wandered 40 years in the wilderness, but YHWH continued to care for them, providing food and water, and guiding them with the pillar of cloud by day and the pillar of fire by night. In spite of this, they continued to worship idols and sacrifice to other gods as spoken of by Stephen (quoting Amos) just before he was stoned to death:

> . . .as it is written in the book of the prophets, "it was not to me that you offered victims and sacrifices forty years in the wilderness, was it, o house of Israel? You also took along the tabernacle of Moloch and the star of the god Rompha, the images which you made to worship. I also will remove you beyond Babylon" (Acts 7:42-43; cf. Amos 5:25).

Idolatry continued throughout their history, even after they had experienced great victories under Joshua in the land of their inheritance, the deliverances accomplished by the judges, and those during the era of the monarchy. Even up to the brink of exile, the writer of Second Kings, in a lengthy description, portrays the extent of Israel's idolatrous practices, which were subject to the last great pre-exilic reform under the reign of King Josiah. The zeal for God, singleness of heart, and thoroughness of actions exhibited by this great king are worthy of attention:

Then the king [Josiah] commanded Hilkiah the high priest and the priests of the second order and the doorkeepers, to bring out of the temple of the LORD all the vessels that were made for Baal, for Asherah, and for all the host of heaven; and he burned them outside Jerusalem in the fields of the Kidron, and carried their ashes to Bethel. He did away with the idolatrous priests whom the kings of Judah had appointed to burn incense in the high places in the cities of Judah and in the surrounding area of Jerusalem, also those who burned incense to Baal, to the sun and to the moon and to the constellations and to all the host of heaven. He brought out the Asherah from the house of the LORD outside Jerusalem to the brook Kidron, and burned it at the brook Kidron, and ground it to dust, and threw its dust on the graves of the common people. He also broke down the houses of the male cult prostitutes which were in the house of the LORD, where the women were weaving hangings for the Asherah . . .

He also defiled Topheth, which is in the valley of the son of Hinnom, that no man might make his son or his daughter pass through the fire for Molech. He did away with the horses which the kings of Judah had given to the sun, at the entrance of the house of the LORD, by the chamber of Nathan-melech the official, which was in the precincts; and he burned the chariots of the sun with fire. . .

The high places which were before Jerusalem, which were on the right of the mount of destruction which Solomon the king of Israel had built for Ashtoreth the abomination of the Sidonians, and for Chemosh the abomination of Moab, and for Milcom the abomination of the sons of Ammon, the king defiled. He broke in pieces the sacred pillars and cut down the Asherim and filled their places with human bones. Furthermore, the altar that was at Bethel and the high place which Jeroboam the son of Nebat, who made Israel sin, had made, even that altar and the high place he broke down. Then he demolished its stones, ground them to dust, and burned the Asherah. . .

Josiah also removed all the houses of the high places which were in the cities of Samaria, which the kings of Israel had made provoking the LORD; and he did to them just as he had done in Bethel. All the priests of the high places who were there he slaughtered on the altars and burned human bones on them; then he returned to Jerusalem (Selected texts from 2 Kings 23:1-25).

Now, in Zechariah's day, God's people had been released from the chains of exile in Babylon and purged of that idolatry. However, this time they did not bring with them idols of stone and wood, but *a spirit*. That spirit had to be deported back to Babylon because it was an infectious disease among the people of God. Its objective was to usurp the authority of the community's true light - the word of God - and replace it, or at least pollute it, with the greedy, self-serving commercial spirit that characterized the culture from which they had been delivered. This issue went far beyond the need for purging of the personal, internal tendencies of individuals as seen in the previous vision. *YHWH was identifying the spirit that influenced the cultural character of the entire nation.* They were living the wrong story – being taught by the wrong narrative. The fact of their total unawareness of it again requires a sovereign act of grace to reveal and remove this influence from among God's heritage. How the deportation of that spirit actually occurred in history is uncertain, but the meaning is clear, a division had to occur which separated (whether spiritually or physically) those who worshipped YHWH in truth from those who served the harlot religion of greed and self-interest. This was finally and definitively accomplished when the nation split over the recognition of Jesus as the Messiah of the Jews – which continues to this day.

THE CHAINS OF CULTURAL HERITAGE

The spirit was lifted and carried off by two female stork-like creatures, probably angels sent to "gather out of his kingdom all stumbling blocks…" (Matthew 13:41) to be removed to, and enshrined in the land of *Shinar*, which, according to the *International Standard Bible Encyclopedia*, was the region immediately surrounding the great city of *Babylon*.

> In Genesis 10:10 it is the district wherein lay Babel, Erech, Accad, and
> Calneh, cities which were the "beginning" of Nimrod's kingdom. In
> Genesis 11:2 Shinar is described as the land of the plain where mi-
> grants from the East settled, and founded Babel, the city, and its great
> tower (International Standard Bible Encyclopedia: e-Sword® edition).

Again, our attention is turned to the significant relationship between Israel and Babylon. We remind ourselves that *Babylon is Israel's
own cultural heritage*. It was out of *Ur of the Chaldeans* (Babylonians)
that the patriarch Abraham was called of God (Genesis 15:7). Now
the power that guided Babylon in wickedness had been unwittingly
carried by God's people as they re-entered the land of promise, still
chained to *old cultural norms*.

The unclean spirit, the spirit of harlotry, was not destroyed in
this vision but confined and removed to be served by those who chose
to remain in Babylon. Those who made the journey to the land of
promise with the vision to build the house of God and restore his city
needed to learn that there would be a severing of all ties to the origins
of their former life. That meant that their new life in the land would be
lived entirely unto YHWH and that there would be no other loyalties
permitted. Therefore, accompanying the postexilic re-establishment
of God's theocratic order was the promised removal of the unclean
spirit which occupied and sought to usurp God's place in the covenant
realm. This removal is further clarified by Zechariah 13 and would
ultimately be fulfilled in the life and ministry of Jesus:

> "It will come about in that day," declares the LORD of hosts, "that
> I will cut off the names of the idols from the land, and they will no
> longer be remembered; and *I will also remove the prophets and the
> unclean spirit from the land*' (Zechariah 13:2).

> "Now when the unclean spirit goes out of a man, it passes through
> waterless places seeking rest, and does not find it. Then it says, "I

will return to my house from which I came"; and when it comes, it finds it unoccupied, swept, and put in order. Then it goes and takes along with it seven other spirits more wicked than itself, and they go in and live there; and the last state of that man becomes worse than the first. That is the way *it will also be with this evil generation*" (Matthew 12:43-45).

The harlot spirit was not destroyed but carried off to Babylon (either literally or figuratively), and enthroned there to be worshipped. Those Israelites who wished to remain her loyal subjects chose a religion of human and national self-interest over worship and service to YHWH and his eternal purposes. Those who chose the harlot had no place in their theology for a poor carpenter from Nazareth who claimed to be their Messiah, especially when it became evident that he had no intention of serving the national interests of a people waiting for him to overthrow Rome.

A final element of the vision is that the woman *filled up* the ephah. In the Greek translation of this text, the translators of the Septuagint used the Greek word *metron* to capture the meaning of the Hebrew word, *ephah*. It is the same Greek word employed in the gospel when Jesus condemned the hypocrisy of the Pharisees:

Fill up, then, the *measure [metron]* of the guilt of your fathers (Matthew 23:32).

It was the harlot spirit that led the nation to not only reject their own Messiah but also to crucify him and persecute the apostles that were sent after him. Everything in the law of Moses, the prophets, and the writings of the Old Testament pointed to the coming of Christ and what he would accomplish among men. However, "He came unto his own and his own did not receive him" (John 1:11). Instead, they chose to *fill up the "bushel" of their guilt* and enthrone the counterfeit based upon traditions, fables, hypocrisy, commercialism, nationalism, and widespread self-interest. That counterfeit would ultimately result in the destruction of their city and temple by the Romans in 70 A.D. – which was the final outcome of their unbelief. Several centuries later, the *Babylonian* Talmud would emerge the single most prestigious compilation of Jewish laws and customs. I find *Babylon* to be a rather fascinating place of its origin.

CONTEMPORARY RELEVANCE

Just as there are latent tendencies or hindrances within us (internal) that must be purged from within us, there are also *external* hindrances – spiritual forces in the world - promoting religion, lust, greed, that these unseen powers continuously seek to sow among the people of God:

> Jesus presented another parable to them, saying, "The kingdom of heaven may be compared to a man who sowed good seed in his field. But while his men were sleeping, his enemy came and sowed tares among the wheat, and went away" (Matthew 13:24-25).

When these exert their influence among God's people, they challenge God's kingdom values, often under the guise of religion, seeking to replace them or diffuse them by merging them with their own. This compromises the people of God to the extent that though we may be worshiping God on Sunday our lives are guided by the same basic values as the fallen world around us. Zechariah's description of the woman was clearly designed to evoke images of dark forces of commercialism and trade as characteristic traits of the harlot spirit. That spirit was one that promoted service to Mammon and had to be removed:

> Thus where Judah had been exiled was a fitting place for wickedness to be worshipped, but not in the land where God had placed his name. The idolatry of Babylon must once and for all be separated from the worship of the God of Israel (Ellison 1979:1034).

1. The spirit of Babylon is a *merchandising* spirit which appears to be symbolized first by the *ephah*, which was used in *trade* and *commerce*; and second, by the *lead cover* which some have suggested is a symbol of *coinage*. Jesus later identified this in the temple where, as he cleansed it from the moneychangers, the buyers, and the sellers:

> And Jesus entered the temple and drove out all who sold and bought in the temple, and he overturned the tables of the money-changers and the seats of those who sold pigeons (Matthew 21:12)

There is no possibility of peaceful coexistence. When commercialism finds its way into the church's life, it infects the people of God with a subtle, but very real money motivation. Everything becomes tainted by profit-making. Church success is measured by collections and building projects. Individual "spirituality," even faithfulness is measured in terms of personal wealth and possessions —assumed to be evidences of God's favor – but yet more, it breeds a religion of *convenience*. Jesus not only drove out the sellers and the money changers, but the *buyers* of their services. Money buys convenience. Many who did not wish to take of their own flocks and journey to Jerusalem for the festivals would merely purchase their sacrifices in Jerusalem. This culture of greed identified in Zechariah remained to the very time of Jesus, but who is to say it is not lurking in the secret places of our Christian communities today? It creates demands on the local church to ensure its members have all the conveniences necessary. Rather than all of us focusing on have something to "bring" to the feast, we pay others to do the work and keep our experience as convenient and unencumbered as possible.

Greed causes the people of God to lose their perspective of the kingdom value of economic justice which ensures that no members of the body lack any basic necessities, and become self-serving in our financial lives. As to its primacy of its dangers, Jesus gave a stern warning to a man who wanted Jesus to intervene in matters concerning an estate:

> Someone in the crowd said to Him, "Teacher, tell my brother to divide the family inheritance with me." But He said to him, "Man, who appointed me a judge or arbitrator over you. Then He said to them, "Beware, and be on your guard against every form of greed; for not even when one has an abundance does his life consist of his possessions" (Luke 12:13-15).

He went on to share a parable about a man who had worked all his life to build reserves for his retirement and contemplated building bigger storage units to preserve his abundance for future use:

> "But God said to him, 'You fool! This very night your soul is required of you; and now who will own what you have prepared?' So is the man who stores up treasure for himself, and is not rich toward God" (Luke 12:20-21).

Jesus makes a clear distinction in this lesson that there are but two options available to us: either we will gather and store *for ourselves*, or we will gather and store up treasures *for the kingdom*. Gathering for the kingdom means to shake ourselves free from anxiety over money, learning to live modestly in a spirit of contentment with what we have and giving generously to those who lack; especially to the needs of God's household. Notice how the apostle Paul sanctifies the basic human activity of work, not emphasizing our personal needs, but those of others:

> He who steals must steal no longer; but rather he must labor, performing with his own hands what is good, *so that he will have something to share with one who has need* (Ephesians 4:28).

> I have coveted no one's silver or gold or clothes. You yourselves know that these hands ministered to my own needs *and to the men who were with me* (Acts 20:33-34).

He also warns about greed as a form of idolatry, which is the rendering of our service to Mammon, hindering our inheritance of the kingdom:

> For this you know with certainty, that no immoral or impure person or *covetous man, who is an idolater,* has an inheritance in the kingdom of Christ and God (Ephesians 5:5).

Mammon seeks to secure what belongs to God – our affections and service - for itself, and is therefore idolatry. In Paul's eyes it is no different than bowing down before a wood carving of an ancient deity.

2. The spirit of Babylon is also a *syncretistic spirit.* Syncretism is a term used to describe the *combination* of different forms of belief or practice. Zechariah was afforded a brief glimpse as the lead cover was lifted enough for him to see inside, and then it was abruptly closed upon the wicked spirit. This, said the angel, was "their appearance in all the land." Israel did not bring idols out of Babylon but a spirit which sought to merge the culture of Babylon with the worship of YHWH. It is no small matter that the name Babylon means *confusion or mixture* (Hitchcock 1869). This enticing spirit attempts to undermine the *critical harmony between worship and behavior.* In Daniel's account of Nebuchadnezzar of Babylon's great statue, built for idolatrous worship, there was *no requirement for character or ethical standards*, only to engage in the act of worship when the music commenced:

> Then the herald loudly proclaimed: "To you the command is given, O peoples, nations, and men of every language, that at the moment you hear the sound of the horn, flute, lyre, trigon, psaltery, bagpipe, and all kinds of music, you are to fall down and worship the golden image that Nebuchadnezzar the king has set up. But whoever does not fall down and worship shall immediately be cast into the midst of a furnace of blazing fire" (Daniel 3:4-6).

Exuberance and charismatic experiences in our worship services may uplift us emotionally, even challenge us spiritually - but ultimately, the community of Christ must live out together at street level a demonstration of the gospel at work as an alternative culture. The gospel is no more compatible with western capitalism than it is socialism or any other socio-economic system. We are called, not merely to participate in "church," as important as that may be, but to live out kingdom values. This is what is meant by the Lord's Prayer, "Your kingdom come. Your will be done, on earth as it is in heaven" (Matthew 6:10). His kingdom comes when the community of faith is a living expression of the character, values, and rule of heaven *and heaven alone*.

The syncretistic spirit influences the people of God to cling to the values of their host culture - merging them with, or mistaking them for kingdom values. This influence has caused many Christians in America to see this country as a "new Israel," or "God's chosen nation," creating an unfortunate combination of loyalties (e. g. "God and country") that assumes that God is on the side of our values and in opposition to the values of other countries. This is not to promote or even suggest an anti-American attitude. As an American citizen, I appreciate the soil upon which I live and the freedoms that God has afforded me us a result of that citizenship, but ultimately, there is only one allegiance for the people of God, and that is *his* kingdom:

> *For our citizenship is in heaven,* from which also we eagerly wait for a Savior, the Lord Jesus Christ..." (Philippians 3:20).

The people of God have engaged in the alignment of themselves along political party lines, foolishly assuming the answers to the country's problems come from within the political process. Unfortunately they do not. It is God who both raises a nation and breaks a nation for his own purposes:

> Behold, the nations are like a drop from a bucket,
> And are regarded as a speck of dust on the scales;
> Behold, He lifts up the islands like fine dust.

Even Lebanon is not enough to burn,
Nor its beasts enough for a burnt offering.
All the nations are as nothing before Him,
They are regarded by Him as less than nothing
and meaningless. . .
It is He who sits above the circle of the earth,
And its inhabitants are like grasshoppers,
Who stretches out the heavens like a curtain
And spreads them out like a tent to dwell in.
He it is who reduces rulers to nothing,
Who makes the judges of the earth meaningless.
Scarcely have they been planted,
Scarcely have they been sown,
Scarcely has their stock taken root in the earth,
But He merely blows on them, and they wither,
And the storm carries them away like stubble (Isaiah 40:15-17,
22-24).

The *one enduring nation* that God has established is that which was born through the cross of Jesus Christ, which is his Church. The Church operates as the *new creation*, under the government of God's kingdom principles, through the agency of the Holy Spirit. It derives its fundamental existence and identity from nothing other than the finished work of Christ. All other agents of human social engineering create ideologies that ultimately prove to be self-serving and idolatrous. The blending of nationalism and kingdom values constitutes spiritual harlotry, which is the reason the Great Harlot of Revelation 17 is referred to as "*Mystery* Babylon."

And he carried me away in the Spirit into a wilderness; and I saw a woman sitting on a scarlet beast, full of blasphemous names, having seven heads and ten horns. The woman was clothed in purple and scarlet, and adorned with gold and precious stones and pearls, having in her hand a gold cup full of abominations and of the unclean things of her immorality, *and on her forehead a name was written, a*

mystery, "Babylon the great, the mother of harlots and of the abominations of the earth" (Revelation 17:3-5).

Mysteries in the Bible often refer to the phenomenon of *two becom-
ing one.* The *incarnation* is called is a mystery because deity and human-
ity became *one being* in the Lord Jesus (1 Timothy 3:16). Paul refers to
marriage as a mystery because husband and wife (representing Christ
and the Church) become *one flesh* (Ephesians 5:32). The formation of
one body or *one new man* in Christ out of two people groups (Jew and
Gentile) is seen as a mystery in Ephesians 3:8. When human culture,
values, religion, commercialism, self-interest, and worldly measures of
success find a home in the community of faith, two cultures are blend-
ed, and *mystery* Babylon is alive and well in our generation.

Chapter 8

THE EIGHTH VISION
CHARIOTS FROM THE THRONE

The purging process having been completed within the covenant realm, the prophet's attention was turned to an eighth and final scene which would involve YHWH's vindication of his name among the nations. Zechariah saw a vision of four chariots proceeding from between two bronze mountains. The chariots were being dispatched to execute his vengeance in regions north and the south of the land of Israel.

Now I lifted up my eyes again and looked, and behold, four chariots were coming forth from between the two mountains; and the mountains were bronze mountains. With the first chariot were red horses, with the second chariot black horses, with the third chariot white horses, and with the fourth chariot strong dappled horses. Then I spoke and said to the angel who was speaking with me, "What are these, my lord?" The angel replied to me, "These are the four spirits of heaven, going forth after standing before the Lord of all the earth, with one of which the black horses are going forth to the north country; and the white ones go forth after them, while the dappled ones go forth to the south country." When the strong ones went out, they were eager to go to patrol the earth. And He said, "Go, patrol the earth." So they patrolled the earth. Then He cried out to me and spoke to me saying, "See, those who are going to the land of the north have appeased my wrath in the land of the north" (Zechariah 6:1-8).

THE CHARIOTS

In this vision, similar to his first, Zechariah saw four messenger-horsemen. In the first vision, the messengers were sent to patrol and report on the state of things and keep watch over the fragile people of God. In this eighth and final vision, the prophet sees *chariots*, which were typically employed in warfare. The different colors of the horses are most likely symbolic of their missions as we saw in Zechariah's first vision and John's vision in Revelation 6. In this scene, the time had come for YHWH to arise and avenge himself and his people. Like the kings of the earth, he has at his disposal thousands of chariots which engage his enemies at his command.

> The chariots of God are myriads, thousands upon thousands;
> The Lord is among them as at Sinai, in holiness (Psalm 68:17).

> Then you will see this, and your heart will be glad,
> And your bones will flourish like the new grass;
> And the hand of the LORD will be made known to His servants,
> But He will be indignant toward His enemies.
> For behold, the LORD will come in fire
> And His chariots like the whirlwind,
> To render His anger with fury,
> And His rebuke with flames of fire (Isaiah 66:14-15).

On the immediate horizon was the pending destruction of the city of Babylon by Darius around 515 B.C. The chariots were being dispatched to the "land of the north" which is the designation of *Babylon* in Zechariah 2:6-7. Because of the clearly stated timeframe of these visions as given to us by Zechariah in chapter 1, we can be reasonably certain that the fall of the city of Babylon is in view in this vision. Twenty years earlier, Cyrus had conquered Babylon and taken the city captive but did not destroy it. He chose rather to preserve it as his own capital. Although Persia conquered the Babylonian Empire and became the foremost power in the civilized world, the capital city of Babylon still remained intact as a towering emblem of human arrogance in the face of YHWH. However, God was not finished with his plans to execute his judgments upon the city. The armies of Darius of

Persia were merely the earthly instruments of the heavenly movement of angelic power. The *Day of the Lord* was fast approaching for YHWH to fulfill the ancient prophetic word of Jeremiah:

For neither Israel nor Judah has been forsaken
By his God, the LORD of hosts,
Although their land is full of guilt
Before the Holy One of Israel.
Flee from the midst of Babylon,
And each of you save his life!
Do not be destroyed in her punishment,
For this is the LORD'S time of vengeance;
He is going to render recompense to her (Jeremiah 51:5-6).

Keil & Delitzsch indicate that there was a historical revolt by Babylon in the time of Darius:

...that the chariot with the horses of the imperial monarchy of Medo-Persia goes to the north country, viz., Mesopotamia, the seat of Babel, to convey the judgment of God thither; that the judgment was at that very time in process of execution, and the chariot was going in the prophet's own day. But although the revolt of Babylon in the time of Darius, and its result, furnish an apparent proof that the power of the Babylonian empire was not yet completely destroyed in Zechariah's time (Keil & Delitzsch: e-Sword® edition).

They also identify Egypt in the south as the destination of the other chariots:

The land of the north, i.e., the territory covered by the lands of the Euphrates and Tigris, and the land of the south, i.e., Egypt, are *mentioned as the two principal seats of the power of the world in its hostility to Israel.* Egypt on the one hand, and Asshur-Babel on the other, which were the principal foes of the people of God, not only before the captivity, but also afterwards, in the conflicts between Syria and Egypt for the possession of Palestine... (Keil & Delitzsch: e-Sword® edition).

THE TWO BRONZE MOUNTAINS

The bronze mountains from which the chariots go forth provide a stunning image with which one may exercise a great deal of interpretive imagination. Historically, we know the image of a *sun-god* rising between two mountains was an ancient pagan symbol of the gate to the underworld.

> Similar symbolism of deities associated with a pair of cosmic mountains is found in near Eastern mythological traditions. The sun-god is represented as appearing between two mountains, and two mountains mark the point of access to the realm of the netherworld deity. . . . The concept conveyed. . .is that of chariots of war passing through the boundary gate of heaven and earth, dispatched by the heavenly Suzerain [Sovereign]-judge on an earthly mission of world judgment (Kline 2001:204).

This image is also suggested in the Book of Malachi:

> But for you who fear my name, the *sun of righteousness will rise* with healing in its wings; and you will go forth and skip about like calves from the stall (Malachi 4:2).

The vision conveyed to Zechariah suggests the same or at least similar imagery, but indicates that the chariots were proceeding from "before the Lord." The vision, therefore, suggests that the two mountains portrayed the towering spectacle of **YHWH** *seated upon his throne, using the earth as his footstool.* The great mountains of bronze were **YHWH**'s *legs* and *feet*, from which the stationed chariots in this vision were dispatched:

> Thus says the LORD, "Heaven is my throne and the earth is my footstool. Where then is a house you could build for me? And where is a place that I may rest?" (Isaiah 66:1).

In the visions of the great prophets, Ezekiel, Daniel, and the apostle John, there is special attention given to God's lower extremities:

It came about in the sixth year, on the fifth day of the sixth month, as I was sitting in my house with the elders of Judah sitting before me, that the hand of the Lord GOD fell on me there. Then I looked, and behold, a likeness as the appearance of a man; *from His loins and downward there was the appearance of fire,* and from His loins and upward the appearance of brightness, like the appearance of glowing metal (Ezekiel 8:1-2).

I lifted my eyes and looked, and behold, there was a certain man dressed in linen, whose waist was girded with a belt of pure gold of Uphaz. His body also was like beryl, his face had the appearance of lightning, his eyes were like flaming torches, *his arms and feet like the gleam of polished bronze,* and the sound of his words like the sound of a tumult (Daniel 10:5-6).

And in the middle of the lampstands I saw one like a son of man, clothed in a robe reaching to the feet, and girded across His chest with a golden sash. His head and His hair were white like white wool, like snow; and His eyes were like a flame of fire. *His feet were like burnished bronze,* when it has been made to glow in a furnace, and His voice was like the sound of many waters (Revelation 1:13-15).

The earlier development of this imagery is found in 1 Kings 7:15-16, which describes the two molten bronze pillars that stood at the entrance of Solomon's Temple:

He fashioned the two pillars of bronze; eighteen cubits was the height of one pillar, and a line of twelve cubits measured the circumference of both. He also made two capitals of molten bronze to set on the tops of the pillars; the height of the one capital was five cubits and the height of the other capital was five cubits (1 Kings 7:15-16).

Again, Meredith Kline has observed:

> We may also recall here the related symbolism of the two bronze pillars (lit. "Standing things") at the temple entrance (1 Kings 7:13-22). In this gate of heaven symbolism, the two bronze pillars represented the side columns, and architectural translation of the anthropomorphic image [having human form] of the bronze legs of deity standing on the Earth . . . Indeed, the elusive connections we have noted indicate that the two bronze mountains *represent the resplendent Lord as planting his feet on the Earth* taking his stand in the midst of his people (Kline 2001:206).

Finally, the Song of Songs gives us an image of the legs of the royal groom as *pillars*:

> His legs are pillars of alabaster set on pedestals of pure gold; his appearance is like Lebanon choice as the cedars (Song of Songs 5:15).

CONTEMPORARY RELEVANCE

1. Each of the two horsemen visions offers a different perspective. The horsemen in the first vision (Zechariah 1:8-12) assured us of God's *omniscience*. As the *all-knowing one*, he is able to patrol the world and is well aware of the events on the ground. This second group, which includes chariots, adds the assurance of God's *omnipotence* - that he is the *all-powerful*, sovereign king, and mighty warrior, able to execute vengeance and exhibit his power when necessary (Meyers 1987:318).

2. Especially noteworthy in this last vision, however, is the mention that the chariot-messengers were, "going forth *after* standing before the Lord of all the earth." This is a valuable insight into the spiritual posture of those of us who would be God's *sent ones*. How often we desire to go forth to do his bidding without having learned to first *stand before the Lord*. The Hebrew text also indicates a sense of *stationing oneself*, or *taking one's stand at the side of*, as opposed to *being placed* there by someone else (Meyers 1987:323). The placing of ourselves before the Lord

is a conscious choice we must make daily to pray, seek his face, and study his word. When our lives are postured in that manner, we can be sent out from his presence with true authority to act on his behalf. As Christians we know that there is "power in his name," which indeed there is. However, the exercise of power of that name comes from *within* a person or community truly acting in accordance with his will, not merely verbalizing the name of Jesus as if it were a magic formula to be invoked. In a well-known biblical narrative, the demons knew Jesus, and they knew Paul, but they recognized that sons of Sceva were acting without divine orders resulting in undesirable consequences for the exorcists:

> But also some of the Jewish exorcists, who went from place to place, attempted to name over those who had the evil spirits the name of the Lord Jesus, saying, "I adjure you by Jesus whom Paul preaches." Seven sons of one Sceva, a Jewish chief priest, were doing this. And the evil spirit answered and said to them, "I recognize Jesus, and I know about Paul, but who are you?" And the man, in whom was the evil spirit, leaped on them and subdued all of them and overpowered them, so that they fled out of that house naked and wounded (Acts 19:13-16).

3. As we have observed, the sequence of Zechariah's visions is no mere coincidence. There is nothing random about what he saw or the order in which they were presented to him. In this final vision, YHWH was moving out to execute vengeance upon his enemies. Whereas the previous lessons were predominantly centered on the community of faith *within* the covenant realm and the throne room, the actions of this final vision are targeted at those *outside*. It suggests to us that the judgment upon Babylon had to wait until after God had *first realigned his own people* to his purposes through judgment:

> For it is time for judgment to begin with the household of God; and *if it begins with us first,* what will be the outcome for those who do not obey the gospel of God? (1 Peter 4:17).

For the weapons of our warfare are not of the flesh, but divinely powerful for the destruction of fortresses. We are destroying speculations and every lofty thing raised up against the knowledge of God, and we are taking every thought captive to the obedience of Christ, and we are ready to punish all disobedience, *whenever your obedience is complete* (2 Corinthians 10:4-6).

God is always at work in and on behalf of his Church. Whether nations, economies, or rulers are shaken, rise, or fall, God has one purpose in mind: the glorification of his son in a perfected Church. We are his masterpiece, being placed on display before powers and principalities (Ephesians 3:10) in order to demonstrate his wisdom and establish his dominion on the earth. However, it is necessary to first bring his own people into alignment with his throne to establish his *base of operations*. In the Old Testament world, that base was the temple. Once the people of God renewed their vision to rebuild the house that bore his name, his throne was again reestablished from which he would execute vengeance upon his enemies.

All of the previous visions were leading up to this point. The work of redeeming, teaching, purging, redefining, and enlarging were all part of the plan to reestablish the reign of YHWH in the midst of a purified people. Once that divine realignment had occurred in the remnant of his people, YHWH was again enthroned in his rightful place. Now, without the aid of an Israelite king, a standing army, or the political machinery of times past, he would again demonstrate his power to both lead his people and deliver them from their enemies.

Both prophets [Haggai and Zechariah] were in agreement, then, that God was about to effect a radical change in the set up of the kingdoms of the earth, an overhaul of the structure and power of the elite nations due to the misappropriation of their resources for their own self-interest and due to their attitude and lack of concern for the ways and people of God…The returned exiles, therefore, should rest content in knowing that the new start God has given them will go unhindered and unopposed by their previous enemies who will soon have their strength removed from them (Smith 2010).

One might think that this is a fitting conclusion, but there was yet one more revelation to be given to the prophet. More needed to be said, and rightly so, concerning the Branch of the Lord, who was first spoken of in Zechariah's throne room vision in Zechariah 3.

HE WILL BRANCH OUT

The word of the LORD also came to me, saying, "Take an offering from the exiles, from Heldai, Tobijah and Jedaiah; and you go the same day and enter the house of Josiah the son of Zephaniah, where they have arrived from Babylon. Take silver and gold, make an ornate crown and set it on the head of Joshua the son of Jehozadak, the high priest."

" Then say to him, 'Thus says the LORD of hosts,' "Behold, a man whose name is Branch, for He will branch out from where He is; and He will build the temple of the LORD. Yes, it is He who will build the temple of the LORD, and He who will bear the honor and sit and rule on His throne. Thus, He will be a priest on His throne, and the counsel of peace will be between the two offices. Now the crown will become a reminder in the temple of the LORD to Helem, Tobijah, Jedaiah and Hen the son of Zephaniah. Those who are far off will come and build the temple of the LORD. Then you will know that the LORD of hosts has sent me to you. And it will take place if you completely obey the LORD your God" (Zechariah 6:9-15).

All of Israel's preparations - as described in this series of visions - were not for themselves but to prepare the way for the *Branch of Lord.* Israel was penultimate – next to last. They were but a voice crying in the wilderness; types and shadows of the genuine vine that was yet to come. Joshua, the high priest, was to be crowned not with a high priest's crown (Hebrew: *nezer*), but a king's crown (Hebrew: *ataroth*). His role as the Priest-King was a forward look, symbolizing the one who was yet to come, even Jesus, who would himself bear the honor of those titles. Here, we learn, as in so many other places in Scripture, that the center of God's purposes is not ourselves, but Jesus, the Son of God. YHWH is ever moving, enlarging, and purifying his people to prepare them to be a suitable habitation and reflection of the Lord Jesus. This great universal purpose being accomplished through Israel would result in the knowledge of God "branching out" from the confines of the city of Jerusalem and the land in order to make ready the way of the Lord. He is the builder of God's true temple – a living one – present in every nation under heaven. Many from among the nations would be drawn to the God of Israel and participate in the building of this *living* temple, made up of people joined inseparably - not by race, gender, or socio-economic class - but by the Spirit of the living God who has breathed into them the resurrected life of Jesus. When we, people of God, pass through exile and the crisis of reorientation, God is redefining, recalibrating, and enlarging our lives to keep us focused on and prepared for our place and mission in the world: to demonstrate the beauty, the power, and the love of God who redeemed us by the blood of his son. Our petty wants and desires have no place in this process. We live for one purpose and one purpose alone - to fulfill that mission of God in our generation.

EPILOGUE

The walls of Jerusalem had to come down. The perverted witness of the community of faith through the centuries of monarchical rule had made a mockery of the name of YHWH among the nations. Israel's proud and arrogant exclusivity was in antithesis to the mission to which she was called of God. That mission was to be a blessing to the nations, by humbly bringing to them the knowledge of the one true deity who had showered so much mercy on Israel herself. To the contrary, their way of life became a perversion of what he had intended for them, prompting him to destroy the nation's socio-economic and religious infrastructure and rebuild with a very small and vulnerable remnant. The idolatry and effects of the ill-fated demand for a human king with all of the political machinery and trappings must be no more. Out of the ashes of exile, a people would return and rebuild – not to the model of the past, but to a new reality with enlarged promises and possibilities. After two generations, up sprang a lowly and vulnerable myrtle tree where the great cedar forest called Jerusalem once stood. This redefined community of faith needed to be re-taught to focus on building a place for their God, and not live in fear, because YHWH would protect them from their enemies. The new city (the true one) was to have walls of fire – the presence of God, rather than brick and mortar – where there would be room for both Jew and gentile, bond and free, rich and poor, to share equally in this all inclusive domain. Because of their awareness of the sovereign grace of God which cleansed them from their sin, they would adorn themselves with missional humility toward those outside, offering them the same grace that they had received.

This newly defined nation would see practical holiness as a thing of beauty, a thing to be desired, not despised - so they would welcome the fire of God to spend the night and purge them of those things that are displeasing to God, including the seductions of the harlot spirit who would attempt to bind them to old identities from which they had been delivered. Their God would be the *one and only one* from whom they derived their identity. Their exclusive loyalty would belong to him. Finally, they would be at peace knowing their God was at rest in his domain, enthroned upon the collective hearts of his people, satisfied with the work he had accomplished in them.

As it was for the ancient people of God, so is it with the New Testament community of faith. God communicated all of these things to his people through the visionary journey of the prophet Zechariah, and we also are beneficiaries of his experience. In the first vision, we were moved (through exile) from selfish exclusivity and pride to a place of vulnerability and uncertainty. The second vision taught us that victory is obtained not by human strength or "super saints," but by a company united by the sole desire to build up the people of God. The third vision warned us not to look to the past exclusive and narrow definitions of God's domain where we are only comfortable among those like ourselves, but to be enlarged to see new possibilities of a reconfigured, universal city of God – one without rigid, inflexible walls of stone and mortar. The fourth and fifth visions reminded us that, in ourselves, we have nothing, but are recipients of sovereign grace – a grace that is channeled through the one who removed iniquity from his people in one day - through his cross. That grace which has come to us through the work of Christ is not only for us, but something that we must offer freely to others in a spirit of missional humility. That form of witness is the light that shines seven times brighter than anything that has gone before. Visions six and seven prepared us for further purifying judgments that must come upon what remains. First, there is a baptism of fire which produces practical holiness. Second, the identification and severing of the influential harlot spirit from among us, which attempts to compromise the people of God with commercialism and other enticements that create a dichotomy between worship and lifestyle. Once YHWH's people have been cleansed and prepared, the final vision reveals a base of operations from which the enthroned King of Kings will arise and defeat our enemies, tearing down strongholds of ungodly power in our field of mission.

When the walls of our self-centered, individualistic, and self-righteous world come tumbling down, we are faced with a choice. We may embrace what God is doing to bring about positive change, or resist and remained locked in the world of yesterday - bemoaning our loss. That choice is ours. Finally, one of the last prophets to cry out to Judah just prior to the Babylonian exile was a man named *Habakkuk*. His name translated from the Hebrew is *Embrace*. As is often the case with the prophets, the man embodies the message. We must *embrace* what God is doing, however painful or humiliating it may be in the short term. We must yield ourselves fully to it and let it redefine, enlarge, and carry us through our crisis of reorientation into a world of new possibilities. *Soli Deo Gloria.*

BIBLIOGRAPHY

Baldwin, Joyce G. 1972. *Haggai, Zechariah, Malachi: An Introduction & Commentary*. Downers Grove, IL: Inter-Varsity Press. (Taken from Haggai, Zechariah, Malachi TOTC by Joyce G. Baldwin. Copyright © Joyce G. Baldwin, 1972. Used by permission of InterVarstiy Press, P.O. Box 1400 Downers Grove, IL 60515. www.ivpress.com)

Berlin, A. and Marc Zvi Brettler, editors. 1999. Jewish Publication Society: *The Jewish Study Bible (Tanakh Translation)*. New York, NY: Oxford University Press.

Bright, John. 1953. *The Kingdom of God*. Nashville, TN: Abingdon Press.

Brueggemann, Walter. 2003. *An Introduction to the Old Testament: The Canon and Christian Imagination*. Louisville, KY: Westminster John Knox Press.

Brueggemann, Walter. 2010. *Out of Babylon*. Nashville, TN: Abingdon Press.

Brueggemann, Walter. 2001. *The Prophetic Imagination* (2nd Ed.). Minneapolis, MN: Augsburg Fortress.

Budde, M.L. and R.W Brimlow. 2002. *Christianity Incorporated*. Grand Rapids, MI: Brazos Press.

Campbell, Charles L. 2002. *The Word Before the Powers, An Ethic of Preaching*. Louisville, KY: Westminster John Knox Press.

Chilton, David. 1990 (3rd Printing). *The Days of Vengeance*. Tyler TX: Dominion Press.

Ellison, David. 1979. "Zechariah," in *The New Layman's Bible Commentary*. Grand Rapids, MI: Zondervan. Taken from The New Layman's Bible Commentary by G.C.D. Howley, F.F. Bruce, and H.L. Ellison: General Editors. Copyright © 1979 by Pickering & Inglis: Glasgow, Scotland. Used by permission of Zondervan. www.zondervan.com.

Federoff, Nicholas. 2005. "Talmudic Evidence for the Messiah at 30 C.E." ©windowview.org; http://www.windowview.org/hmny/pgs/talmuds.30ce.html (retrieved 3/10/11)

Fee, Gordon. 1996. *Paul, the Spirit, and the People of God*. Peabody, MA: Hendrickson.

Frost, Michael and Alan Hirsch. 2003. *The Shaping of Things to Come: Innovation and Mission for the 21st-Century Church*. Peabody, MA: Hendrickson

Grenz, Stanley. 1996. *A Primer on Postmodernism*. Grand Rapids, MI: Eerdmans.

Harris, R.L., G. L. Archer, B.K. Waltke Jr. 1980. *Theological Wordbook of the Old Testament-Vol. II*. Chicago, IL: Moody Press.

Hauerwas, Stanley. 2001. "Reforming Christian Social Ethics: Ten Theses," in *The Huerwas Reader*. Ed. Hohn Berkman and Michael Cartwright. Durham, NC: Duke University Press

Hitchcock, Roswell D. 1869. "Hitchcock's Bible Names Dictionary" from: *Hitchcock's New and Complete Analysis of the Holy Bible*. e-Sword Edition: e-Sword.exe; Application Version 9.8.0.2 - Downloaded from www.e-Sword.net, © 2000-2011- Rick Meyers.

Jordan, James. 2000. *Through New Eyes*. Eugene, OR: Wipf & Stock.

King James Version of the Bible. 1769. Authorized Version. e-Sword Edition: e-Sword.exe; Application Version 9.8.0.2 - Downloaded from www.e-Sword.net, © 2000-2011- Rick Meyers.

Keil, Johann (C.F.) and F. Delitzsch. *Commentary on the Old Testament.* e-Sword. e-Sword Edition: e-Sword.exe Application Version 9.8.0.2 - downloaded from www.e-Sword.net, © 2000-2011- Rick Meyers.

Klein, W., C. Blomberg, R. Hubbard, Jr. 2004 (2nd ed.). *Introduction to Biblical Interpretation.* Nashville, TN: Thomas Nelson, Inc.

Kline, Meredith G. 2001. *Glory in Our Midst.* Eugene, OR: Wipf and Stock. Used by permission of Wipf and Stock Publishers. www.wipfandstock.com.

Merrill, Eugene. "Zechariah Part 1 - The Night Visions (1:1—6:15)" .2006. Biblical Studies Press. Reprinted with permission from http://bible.org (retrieved 2/10/11).

http://bible.org/seriespage/zechariah-part-1-night-visions-11%E2%80%94615.

Meyers, Carol and Eric Meyers. 1987. *The Anchor Bible: Haggai, Zechariah 1-8 – A New Translation with Introduction and Commentary.* Garden City, NY: Doubleday & Company.

Miller, Fred P. 1999. *Zechariah and Jewish Renewal: From Gloom to Glory - A Commentary on the Book of Zechariah.* MoellerHaus Publisher http://www.moellerhaus.com/ http://www.ao.net/~fmoeller/zec5.htm (retrieved 2/21/11).

Orr, James (Editor). 1939. *The International Bible Encyclopedia.* e-Sword Edition: e-Sword.exe Application Version 9.8.0.2 - downloaded from www.e-Sword.net, © 2000-2011- Rick Meyers.

Peterson, David L. 1995. *Zechariah 9-14 and Malachi.* Louisville, KY: Westminster John Knox Press.

Rotherham, Joseph Bryant. 1902. *The Emphasized Bible.* Grand Rapids, MI: Kregel Publications. (Foreword Copyright 1994 by Kregel Publications)

Smith, Lee. 2010. "Zechariah." In "Old Doctrines, New Light" http://www.arlev.co.uk/zechhome.htmSmith (retrieved 3/2/11 from linked section Zechariah 6:1-8)

Stone, Bryan. 2007. *Evangelism After Christendom*. Grand Rapids, MI: Brazos.

Strong, James, S.T.D., LL.D. 1890. *Strong's Hebrew and Greek Dictionaries*. e-Sword Edition: e-Sword.exe Application Version 9.8.0.2 - downloaded from www.e-Sword.net, © 2000-2011- Rick Meyers.

Whitelam, Keith W. and Robert B. Coote. 1979. *The Just King: Monarchial Judicial Authority in Ancient Israel*. Sheffield: Sheffield Academic Press (JSOT Supplementary Series 12).

Whiston, William (Translator). 1987. *The Works of Josephus – Antiquities of the Jews*. Peabody, MA: Hendricksen Publishers.

Wink, Walter. 1984. *Naming the Powers: The Language of Power in the New Testament*. Philadelphia, PA: Fortress Press.

Wink, Walter. 1986. *Unmasking the Powers*. Philadelphia, PA: Fortress Press.

Young, Robert. 1898 Rev. ed. *Young's Literal Translation of the Bible*. e-Sword Edition: e-Sword.exe Application Version 9.8.0.2 - downloaded from www.e-Sword.net, © 2000-2011- Rick Meyers.